One Doctor's Story

One Doctor's Story

◆

From the Hills of West Virginia to Washington, D.C.

John F. J. Clark, Jr., MD

with Gwendolyn Scotton Bethea

iUniverse, Inc.
New York Lincoln Shanghai

One Doctor's Story
From the Hills of West Virginia to Washington, D.C.

iUniverse, Inc.

For information address:
iUniverse, Inc.
2021 Pine Lake Road, Suite 100
Lincoln, NE 68512
www.iuniverse.com

ISBN: 0-595-32929-2

Printed in the United States of America

This book is dedicated to my wives.

To my late wife, Adelaide, whose support over fifty years of marriage enabled me to commit my life to the practice of medicine. To my wife, Alberta, who has acted as a sounding board during the past five years that went into the making of this book.

Contents

Preface

I have written this book during a time when America's families are experiencing a revived interest in the histories of their own and other families that make up the United States; families whose backgrounds are as rich as they are diverse. Among African Americans, family backgrounds are as varied as the myriad paths upon which we have come. Although African Americans have a common ancestry, these paths have followed many twists and turns—guided by the area of the country in which family roots have been planted, and sometimes by sheer human willpower and the unique circumstances of our birth.

This book also comes at a time when the health disparities between African Americans and the broader society continue to be of grave concern. It is a time when diseases and illness associated with the maternal health of adult women are increasingly being diagnosed in adolescents, particularly among African Americans.

My political and social views on life and on the medical field in particular, were greatly shaped by my environment and education as a child in Charleston, West Virginia, and expanded as I reached adulthood and became a medical doctor in Washington, D.C.

There was a huge difference in the environments of Charleston and Washington, D.C., but what the two cities had in common—complete racial segregation—meant that Black people in both cities experienced rampant racism. In the aftermath of segregation and the struggle for civil rights, today both cities offer numerous opportunities for their residents, including blacks and other minorities.

During my youth, however, medical care for African Americans in Charleston was so horrible that people were afraid to go to the hospitals because of the segregationist policies. Blacks were treated in basements, and often ended up in morgues. Moreover, the incidents of maternity mortality and infectious disease, such as tuberculosis, were highest among the black population.

There were very few black doctors, especially in specialties such as surgery, internal medicine, gynecology, pediatrics and internal medicine. Because of the atmosphere, I had no real role models, especially among specialists in obstetrics and gynecology. The only black doctors were family practitioners. This made me very eager to become a specialist in medicine and an educator. I saw this as my opportunity to contribute to a solution of the problems brought on by the lack of highly trained black physicians.

When I was accepted into Howard University's medical school on my birthday, December 8, it was the best gift I could have received. It seemed to me, I was destined to fulfill my goals in life at Howard. Though I was accepted into several other schools, I chose to follow my oldest sister, Dr. Lucille Clark, who was a third year medical student at Howard the year I arrived.

As a student I was often embarrassed and angered by the segregation in the medical field, especially as it manifested itself in Washington, D.C. One of the worst examples was the way in which black medical students were treated when we visited D.C. General Hospital. When I was a medical student from 1943 to 1946, the black students could only visit D.C. General—as if we were taking a trip to the zoo. We were allowed to look but not touch. When I became chairman of the Obstetrics and Gynecology department at the young age of 35, the situation at D.C. General Hospital was one of the first things I changed. My emphasis was to allow black students training and serving residencies at D.C. General the same access as the students from Georgetown and George Washington universities.

My next concern was to enhance the training of black doctors in obstetrics and gynecology. I increased the training duration from 3 years to 5 years. The number of residents in the program went from 3 to 30. During the 19 years I was chairman, more students from Howard went into OB/GYN than into any other specialty.

At that time, as presently, research data showed maternal mortality to be greater for minorities in America. Then, the global solution was to train midwives throughout Great Britain, Africa and the Caribbean. I did not perceive that to be the best solution for the high mortality rate among minority women. I believed black doctors should be trained to handle childbirth and all birthing problems. Midwives should work as assistants. I began to institute these changes into the medical curriculum.

During the early 1970's, the number of students entering obstetrics and gynecology declined in the leading schools. Immigrants from The Philippines, India, Korea, South Africa and China later met the demand for doctors. The medical departments of these institutions did not see the need to actively recruit black students. Only a token number could be found on the campuses of the predominantly white schools. In the early 1970's there were 71 black doctors in training out of 2,655 total doctors trained. Of those 71 doctors, Howard trained *30*. That was a very high discrepancy. The problem is discussed in a later chapter of this book and in articles in the Appendix.

Another great concern was abdominal pregnancies, postpartum bleeding, and toxemia. These conditions were among the highest causes of maternal mortality and morbidity in the black population. The research findings of these problems are also discussed briefly later in this book and in articles in the Appendix.

Since I have retired, I am happy to say that the Washington D.C. in which I now live is an integrated city in a neighborhood that was once open only to whites. I am also happy to be part of an integrated medical community that fosters the training and hiring of black doctors. My trainees practice at all the hospitals in the District, Maryland and Virginia, which was unheard of when I first came to Washington, D.C. not that long ago.

In the early 1970's, I was appointed chairman of the Washington, D.C. March of Dimes. Before my tenure, only one hospital in the District received March of Dimes funds. After I made a point of the fact that the March of Dimes was a citywide effort, Howard was included in the disbursement of those community contributions. Following my tenure a member of the Georgetown Medical School took over as chairman.

My family has been and continues to be the greatest influence on my life, but there have been many others who have helped me formulate my views and the tenor of my life.

Individuals such as Booker T. Washington, W. E. B. Dubois, Carter G. Woodson, Leon Sullivan (my high school classmate), Adam Clayton Powell's family, Jesse Owens, Mordecai Wyatt Johnson, Robert Chambliss, Charles Diggs, George Crockett, Paul "Tank" Younger, Jeannine Clark, Frank Smith, Martin Luther King, Jr., Vernon Jordan, Nelson Mandela, Mahatma Gandhi, Franklin D. Roosevelt, Harry Truman, Lyndon B. Johnson, Dan Collins, Winston Churchill, Jesse Jackson, Mary McLeod Bethune, and my great uncle Charles James. My latest influence is my wife, Alberta Clark.

All my life, I have been a student of two topics: propaganda and politics. Unfortunately, I have found these topics have dominated the thought processes and consequent actions of a great many individuals who have either crossed my path or been instrumental in the social/political environment I have observed through the years. Yet, I realize my basic optimism about life has remained unchanged and my goals have remained undeterred.

In this book I have chronicled some early studies in maternal health I conducted alone and with colleagues and students at what was then Freedmen's Hospital, the nation's first hospital dedicated to providing healthcare to black people after the Civil War. Freedmen's later became the world-renowned Howard University Hospital.

This book will hopefully provide a glimpse of the research that was conducted at Howard University Hospital during several decades in the 20th century to help African Americans meet their maternal health care needs. At the same time I chronicled my own family's history and progress, which ultimately inspired me to accomplish whatever I have accomplished in my lifetime.

The chapter on some of the research I conducted either alone or with my colleagues is also a tribute to them as nationally and internationally renowned medical professionals in their own right. Much of this research occurred while I was chairman of the Department of Obstetrics and Gynecology at Howard University College of Medicine. It is also significant as it details the research and the medical conditions of the predominantly black patients of the former Freedmen's Hospital from the late 1950's to the 1970's. It continues through the early period after the name of the hospital was changed to Howard University Hospital, and, as the hospital became one of the nation's preeminent teaching hospitals, especially for African American physicians. This chapter also voices my concern for documenting some medical highlights of a period of time when black women and girls were dying at disproportionate rates from maternal illnesses as compared to the national female population.

I owe everything to my father and mother and to my siblings and wife, whose inspiration and vision helped me to hold fast to my dream. Because of them, whatever success I have can be measured only in terms of helping others.

The obvious aim of this book is to provide a basis for further medical research that must continue to play a significant role in improving the lives of African Americans in particular and for all citizens.

When I look back over my life, I realize everything I previously thought of as a disadvantage was actually an advantage. I am pleased I was able to improve healthcare in the black community, especially for poor black women. I am also grateful I was able to train young black doctors who in turn went back into our communities to practice medicine and others who received national recognition in the medical field. But most of all, I am proud I helped fulfill the dream and vision of two extraordinary people—my mother and father.

Introduction

My grandfather thanks me often for assisting him in writing his memoirs, but I should be thanking him. In the three years we have worked together on this project, I have learned what went into the making of Dr. John F. J. Clark, Jr. and have gained so much pride in him and the family that contributed to the person he has become.

Before working on his memoirs, I thought I knew about my grandfather and his family life in Charleston, West Virginia, having attended events honoring my grandfather's contribution to medicine and listened at family dinners when various members told funny stories of their childhood together. My favorite is when my cousin Stephen tells the one about my great-grandmother Hattie's pony, Nell. Nell was so smart that she would drop my grandmother off at the train station in the morning and like clockwork would return rider-less from the family farm in the evening to pick her up. It wasn't until I sat down and listened to my grandfather tell the story of his life, in his words, that I truly understood the person he is.

My grandfather is a humble man. When we started working on this book it was a story about the Clark family, since he rightly credits his success to his parents' wisdom and his siblings' support. He knows that the person he has become is a direct result of his parents and siblings. It was with much prodding from editorial advisers that he decided to limit this book to his personal memoirs.

My grandfather is a man dedicated to family. He does everything in his power to assist his children, grandchildren, siblings and extended family in successfully achieving their goals.

My grandfather is a man committed to medicine. He dedicated his life to a career in the practice and teaching of obstetrics and gynecology. In his 40 years of teaching, he trained more black doctors than anyone at the time. His tireless effort to increase the number of African American doctors in his field, ending discriminatory practices at local hospitals, and his quest to improve maternal health care (especially for poor blacks) are just some of his notable contributions to medicine. At his 80th birthday celebration, his wife, Alberta, had to limit the number of speakers because so many former students wanted to say a few words about studying under "The Chief." The most interesting thing about their speeches was not their comments about his medical teachings (which were many), but the human aspect he took to teaching. He cared not only that they learned or that they were good doctors, he cared if they were good people and good to their patients.

My grandfather is a man committed to education. Throughout this book you will read of his many accomplishments. None of those accomplishments could have been reached without education. The commitment to education did not begin with him, but with his grandmother, Lucy Clark, who attended Oberlin College and insisted that her son, John Sr. "not become a blacksmith like his father."

My grandfather is a hard working man. Before working on this book, I did not know that my grandfather was dyslexic, that he would get up at 4 o'clock every morning to study, that he taught himself to run track by reading books, that he was the president of his medical class…the list goes on and on.

My grandfather is a great man. His greatness is a direct result of his parents John Sr. and Hattie Clark. They possess all of the character traits I mentioned above and instilled them in their children. Hopefully this memoir will serve as a historical account for those who unfortunately did not have the privilege to have sat with such a great man as he recounted his life.

Nicole R. Clark

1

Ancestors

At twelve, I first realized I wanted to become a doctor. Even at such a young age, I was aware that black people, particularly black women, died disproportionately of preventable illnesses in our town of Charleston, West Virginia. My father's first wife died of an illness associated with childbirth; and my own mother wisely chose to have all of her children—my brother, three sisters and me—at home, rather than be subjected to the poor medical care that blacks often received at the local hospital. More often than not, after being relegated to the basement facilities, blacks all too frequently emerged only to be taken to the morgue.

This is the story of how my youthful dream of being a doctor became a reality and how I spent my professional life contributing whatever I could to enhance the healthcare of blacks, especially black women and ending the discriminatory medical practices that limited the education of black doctors.

This story winds from the slavery of my ancestors, to my childhood in Charleston, to the great and powerful city of Washington, D.C., where I practiced and taught medicine for more than 40 years.

It is my family's story, yet it provides a parallel glimpse into some critical periods in the nation's history and the conditions and lives of the black people who once provided the free labor that transformed this nation from its agrarian origin.

I am sure I inherited my ancestors' extraordinary will and fortitude which allowed me to make a difference in the maternal health of black women, especially poor women with little or no access to good health care. I am fortunate to be able to relay my forefathers' stories through this narrative. Here is our story.

My paternal great grandfather was born a slave on a plantation in North Carolina. He was a barrows builder who became so good at his trade he was able to earn enough money to buy his and his wife's freedom. In the early 1800's my great grandfather and his wife moved from North Carolina to southern Ohio, where their eight sons were born. One of the eight was Ben Franklin Clark, my grandfather.

Although he was born in 1850, 12 years before slavery ended, Ben Franklin Clark never experienced slavery. Still its vestiges hung like a damp enveloping cloud over his life as if he had actually experienced it. Touched by the excitement of the coal mining boom of the late 1800's, Ben, like many other blacks, left Ohio in search of jobs in Charleston, West Virginia, (the center of the booming coal mining industry).

From its early days, the city of Charleston always had fertile rolling hills. The summer harvest yielded fresh peaches and other fruits. The area's new farmers made money from chickens, cattle, and dairy products, but West Virginia was better known in the 1800's for its bituminous coal, metal factories, and steel mills. The state's industrialization expansion in the late 19th century was based on rich resources and supported by the migration of southern blacks and northern laborers

Ben arrived in Charleston after traveling for days on foot. There he found many blacks working as coal miners and as blacksmiths. Eventually, he took up the blacksmith trade and began earning a modest sum, but enough to enjoy a small measure of life's comfort.

Ben married Lucy James, my grandmother, and soon after started their family. Before Lucy met Ben, she applied and was accepted to Oberlin College (1872), one of the few elite colleges for women that admitted blacks. She was one of the first black women to be admitted. Lucy's matriculation at Oberlin was shortened when she married. In the midst of the first years of their marriage, Lucy formed an elementary school for black girls, thus began the Clark teaching tradition that continues today.

Ben and Lucy had two children; John Francis (b.1874) and his sister Mattie (b. 1877). John Francis was my father. Although Ben would eventually own a 108-acre farm, it was passed down orally to future generations that Lucy did not want her son to be a blacksmith like his father. The work was too long, too laborious, and nearly everyone she knew who worked as a blacksmith had little to show for the long hours of toil and sweat. My father showed early signs of superior intelligence as he mastered such subjects as Latin, mathematics, and history. Right from the start, Lucy focused on my father's education and sent him to school in a horse-drawn carriage.

Lucy's ancestors were indentured servants in the first colony, Jamestown, Virginia. Fate or a disguised blessing may be the only explanation for the circumstances that led to the James family earning its freedom. One day, the baby of the owner of the plantation accidentally fell into the James River. A particularly observant family member dove into the river and saved the child from drowning.

Overcome with gratitude, the owner freed the entire James family. Subsequently, they rode to West Virginia on horse and buggy and began a new life devoid of the watchful eyes of a plantation owner and the often-payless toil and sweat of their lives as indentured servants.

Lucy's brother, Charles H. James was known for his extraordinary business acumen. Selling coals from bags he carried on his back, Charles was probably one of the original door-to-door salesmen. He became quite successful just a few decades after the end of slavery. Charles went on to become a wholesale business-man, selling such produce as eggs and vegetables. Only a few years ago, Charles's great grandson sold the business for $25 million. Another of Lucy's brothers grew so disgusted with the plight of blacks in West Virginia that he left for Brazil in 1916 and never returned.

2

John F. J. Clark, Sr.

Being mountainous with small narrow valleys, the geography of West Virginia never lent itself well to slavery. Thus in 1861, West Virginia seceded from Virginia and remained in the Union, fighting on the Union side during the Civil War and considered itself a Border State. It differed from the other states of the South in that it bore no post-war animosity, and it retained its functioning two-party system, particularly in local politics. The white men, who later became the bankers, politicians, big business owners, and mayor, grew up with my mother in the country. This later worked to her advantage during her days as a successful entrepreneur.

Despite the peculiar status of West Virginia, blacks in Charleston held mostly menial jobs or were otherwise adversely affected by the serious labor problems that existed within the mining, steel, and chemical industries. Most blacks in town barely had a grade school education. Therefore, they could not move upward into a fruitful, productive livelihood. They found themselves relegated to jobs by their race and class. My father was determined that he would assist blacks to get better jobs. As he grew into this mindset, *he decided to become a teacher* and enrolled in the University of Chicago.

As one of only a handful of black students, my father graduated from the University of Chicago in 1899. As his mother had hoped, *John would not be a black-smith like his father.* After graduation, my great uncle Charles helped my father move back home to Charleston and offered him a place to stay in his home.

Father accepted a teaching position in the "Negro" school system at Garnet (named after Ambassador Garnett to Liberia) in 1900. At the time, the school system extended only to the eighth grade for Negro youth. Although Garnet High School was established in 1899, it was not until 1909 that the first separate high school building was built. Father accepted a teaching position at the new high school in 1908. After teaching Latin, science, mathematics and English for a number of years, he was appointed principal. During the next 46 years, he became one of the most respected educators in West Virginia. Under his direction, and with the support of a highly qualified staff of 20, Garnet became a first-class senior high school. In 1927, the school was moved into a new building. While father was principal, the majority of Garnet graduates went on to college.

My father received his Master of Education from Harvard in 1925. He earned the degree from one of the nations most elite institutions while taking classes during the summer breaks from Garnet. Consistent with his goal to provide opportunities to uplift blacks with trade education, his Master's thesis topic was, "A Program for Vocational Guidance in Garnet High School."

3

Hattie Peters Clark

My mother, Hattie Peters, was born in Rocky Mountain, Virginia in 1888. She was only five when she traveled to Tupper's Creek, West Virginia. During Hattie's early years, the deadly scourge of tuberculosis was rampant throughout America, particularly within black communities. Although Hattie proved to have a natural immunity, her mother, Elvira Peters and four of her nine siblings did not. They died of the disease.

Blacks in Tupper's Creek were barely able to attain a grade school education, much less graduate from high school or college. Yet despite the harsh realities of life in Tupper's Creek, Hattie set her sights on college

Hattie's great uncle, Byrd Prillerman, was the president of West Virginia State College. He was a man of some financial means and was widely respected in Tupper's Creek. In 1904, Byrd and his wife offered to let Hattie live with them while she attended West Virginia State. Teaching was the only profession to which single women could aspire, so, in the tradition of the era, Hattie earned her teacher certificate at West Virginia State in 1907 and was appointed to a position at the local all black elementary school.

Living with Byrd Prillerman and his wife was an awkward experience since she was treated like a servant rather than a visiting relative. Despite the awkwardness, she was proud of the fact that her uncle was so well respected, and that his home was the meeting place of some of the most influential blacks of the time. Hattie usually caught only a glimpse of those individuals.

Booker T. Washington was one of those visitors. He was the talk of not only West Virginia, but also the entire country for his bold and outspoken views. He established Tuskegee Institute and was a significant influence on the development of West Virginia State College, which was founded 10 years after Tuskegee.

To her amazement, Hattie's Uncle Byrd allowed her to sit at the dinner table and was formally introduced to Washington. Her great aunt wanted her to eat in the kitchen as she normally did. To Hattie, Washington was larger than life, a man of great depth and wisdom, as well as a world renowned educator. Hattie tucked this memory neatly away until the day she relayed it to my siblings and me. I too told the story to my own children and grandchildren.

My mother also loved to tell how Adam Clayton Powell, Sr. (father of the legendary New York legislator Adam Clayton Powell, Jr.) was hidden by her family while he escaped town. He was a minister from Montgomery, West Virginia, who was as outspoken or more so than his son would be and his political and social activism proved too dangerous for him and his family members.

Hattie was inspired by the Prillermans' success in rising above their circumstances to become successful teachers and business people. Following in their footsteps, Hattie cultivated an entrepreneurial spirit and an eye for a good business deal. At the age of 18, when girls' thoughts usually centered on preparing for marriage, Hattie bought a 100-acre farm and helped her father buy a farm as well. Hattie's farm would later become the foundation for the family's wealth (natural gas was discovered on her farm in the 1930's). Parlaying her innate business sense into land ownership and a successful real estate career (the first woman in West Virginia to attain a real estate license), she became one of the most well-to-do women in the state and gained wide respect from both black and white residents of Charleston.

4

Marriage and Childrearing

In 1916, my parents married and began their family, which would consist of three daughters; Lucille (b.1921), Harriette Mae (b.1925), and Carolyn (b.1929) and two sons; me (b.1922) and Charles (b.1926). Growing up in the Clark household revolved around getting a good education and helping others who were less fortunate.

Our mother and father believed education to be the single most important key to success, so there was no question the Clark children would do well in school. Father sat with each of us daily after school to go over homework until he was satisfied that we had completed it to the best of our ability (which was considerably enhanced under his watchful tutelage). Father was a scholar of the classics and he tutored my siblings and me in Greek and Latin.

I was very eager to start school and entered at the age of five. I suffered from dyslexia (then undiagnosed and unheard of), so I had trouble reading. Everyday at 4 o'clock in the morning, my father would awaken me to complete my schoolwork. Even though I excelled at all other subjects except reading, my first grade teacher told my parents I would never get beyond sixth grade. My parents waited to reveal her prediction to me until long past the time it could negatively affect me. When I recall my childhood, the likelihood of not succeeding in school was impossible since the word, "can't" was never part of the Clark vocabulary.

It was a family tradition for each child to read to the younger sibling until that child could read for himself or herself. Although Harriette was the middle child, she was the oldest of the younger three, so mother proclaimed her top dog among the younger children. Harriette believes that she first learned leadership skills while caring for and being in charge of the younger children. When she came home from school, she would set up her own class and teach Charles everything she had leaned that day. It gave Charles a head start he never lost.

My father left the house early enough in the morning to reach school by 6:30 am, when the school buses would start to arrive. Even though there were two school systems under segregation, there was only one set of buses. The black students were picked up first in the morning and brought home last in the evening, meaning our dad did not leave school until 5:30 pm daily. After that kind of day, we really did not want him to come home to a domestic problem. He was stern at school and at home. He used to say he did not like to chew food twice, and that he did not like to give orders. He would spank us boys if we did not move when he said move, but we knew that, so we did, and he didn't.

Father was also a very gentle person. The girls in the family were never punished physically. He often humored Harriette by attending her parties and sipping tea from her doll cups. As our father grew older, he often fell asleep reading in his big chair. Harriette would braid his silky, gray hair that he wore long in the front to hide his bald spot. Of course he would be annoyed when he awoke, because he usually had an evening meeting to attend and would have to comb his hair again.

Although he did spend a great deal of time with us, as an older father, he did not play ball with his sons like some other dads. We were blessed to have three uncles, Roscoe, Tom and Ruby, who spent a great deal of time with us. Our uncles played with us, built us a jungle gym, taught us to drive and generally played a great part in our becoming adults with plenty of interests.

My mother's father, Papa Peters, was another great nurturer of us. Not being able to read or write, he found great satisfaction in being a great storyteller. He would bounce the girls on his knees and enthrall them with tales of Peter Rabbit, and the briar patch. They never tired of them, because he always changed the endings.

Our house was only a few blocks from the *grand mansion* that served as the state capitol. Completed in 1932, the Italian Renaissance designed building was dominated by a 293 foot gilded dome. Throughout our childhood, my sisters, brother and I played together in its shadow. Our mother would say, "never sell our property here on Washington Street (we owned three pieces of property at the time), because one day the capitol is going to move down to you". My siblings and I thought that was the most astonishing thing we had ever heard. We could not imagine a great, big building moving, but Mother was right. Over the years, the adjacent property was purchased to expand the capitol building. Now the capitol is the next-door neighbor to a piece of our land that was once in the middle of the block.

Our next-door neighbors were Jewish, Lebanese, Syrian and German. Although we were on speaking terms, we never experienced a sense of true neighborliness. Since we lived in a predominantly white neighborhood that was impervious to us, our large extended family provided a built-in community under one roof. Growing up, our house was home to five relatives (along with countless others), who were the same age as each Clark child. Each went to school with us. For Lucille, there was Shaffer; for John there was Poindexter; Harriette had Elvira; Charles had Junior; and Carolyn had Carolyn P. That made for plenty of lateral and vertical relationships.

Our days were filled with jumping, romping, skating, and running in our neighbor Aunt Fannie's tennis court. We would play tirelessly until we heard "The Whistle." The Whistle would call us in from play to supper with a shrill persistence that could not be mistaken or ignored.

Since the schools were so small and the teachers knew all the families we felt more like we were attending private schools rather than segregated public school. We walked several miles to reach the elementary school we attended. My siblings and I attended the public high school, Garnet, where our father was principal. With only a few hundred students, it was small by today's standards. Garnet teachers were very attentive. Even though my father was the principal, I received little attention from the teachers compared to other students, yet I managed to receive high academic honors.

Our parents also made sure that we had other interests outside of school. The girls walked to town to learn sewing, a skill considered a must. Since mother was a self-taught botanist, she helped my sisters start their gardens. Each child was required to learn to play the piano. Our teacher, Mrs. Wanza, was a well-trained classical pianist who had studied in Paris. While Lucille and the other siblings excelled in music, I preferred sports.

In high school, I wanted desperately to play football. Small in weight for my height at 126 pounds, I could not match up with other players who were much heavier. At the time, coaches were allowed to take grown men off the street to make up the team. Therefore, I decided to teach myself to run track, since the Garnet coach showed only minimal interest in the sport. I read everything I could get my hands on about track and was particularly intrigued by the athletic feats of Jesse Owens at Ohio State, who dominated track there from 1934 to 1935. He became one of the world's greatest athletes and was the first American in the history of the Olympics to win four gold medals in a single Games event. At Ohio State, he set three world records and tied a fourth at the 1935 Big Ten championships.

I combined my book knowledge and a natural ability to run and jump hurdles higher than most of my competitors, into a successful high school track record. Despite the fact that the coach had not originally wanted the team to go to the state championship due to a disagreement over who would represent the team (the coach wanted to send adults off the street rather than the students who had trained all year), my father ended up taking us to the competition. The team won 14 out of 16 first place medals. I was second in the state, an accomplishment that I would always consider as one of the proudest moments of my youth. I gave my medals to Harriette to keep from having to give them to my girlfriend. She wore them as silver bracelets. One day, she lost the medals on a hiking trip. She still grieves over that even now.

Mother's energy was boundless and she loved to walk. She felt that the street-cars that jingled by our house were for "long trips only." Neither of our parents felt comfortable driving. They had driver's licenses and cars mostly because they believed obtaining the licenses was a right, almost as important as the right to vote. Automobiles did not become a common mode of transportation until my parents were well into adulthood. The children, therefore, were asked often to take the wheel, with Charles or one of our uncles often serving as father's "chauffeur." As we rode along, our dad would use the occasion to dispense words of wisdom, some of which he had tried out previously in speeches to community groups such as the NAACP, where he was regarded as a patriarch. These words of wisdom sometimes came in the form of cornball jokes and sometimes in the form of folk phrases and admonishments. The humor and underlying wisdom of his phrases were not lost on us:

If you lie down with dogs, you'll get up with fleas.
You can't soar with the eagles in the day if you run with foxes at night.
Nothing good comes in bunches but bananas and grapes
If you put your money in your socks, you'll have it in the morning
if you don't take your socks off.
Don't go out with people in the evening
you would not want to be seen with in the daytime.
Don't marry a dumb woman.

We studied through most of our summer vacation—a normal thing for us since father also ran the summer school at Garnet, but we also often traveled to our grandfather Ben's 105-acre farm in Vinton, Ohio. We greatly anticipated the trips to the farm, even though farm life was much different from life in Charleston, notably the outdoor plumbing, the spring and well water, and the rainwater we used for bathing and washing clothes. We grew to love reading by natural sunlight in the daytime and eating by candlelight and kerosene lanterns at night. Charles is particularly fond of his memories of the simplicity of walking down a hill across a highway to a natural "rock spring" to drink cool spring water during the long summer days.

Our Uncle Albert, father's brother-in-law, was a taskmaster who believed daylight was not to be wasted. "If the sun is up, you should be too," was his motto. Yet, as stern as Uncle Albert could be, he was equally fair and was known to have a kind streak, though he rarely showed it. Uncle Albert's wife, Aunt Mattie, was kind and gentle and their daughter, Virginia, loved to tell ghost stories. We would listen intently, and it always felt like *something* was always just behind the bushes, ready to pounce and scare the living daylight out of us. We loved every minute of it.

We also attended special events during the summer. I especially remember the Chicago World's Fair in 1933 (Charles was mesmerized by the electric door) and the New York World's Fair in 1939 (the Garnet school band played). Summer in Chicago was always a convenient place for us to live as our father studied for his PhD at the University of Chicago.

While our family had the good fortune of being able to travel comfortably in our big, dark green, blacktop touring sedan, we, nevertheless, were not immune from the racial segregation of the times. We often packed our own food for the two or three day trips, and stopped along the roadside or at a suitable grassy spot to spread out our picnic lunch; all because the local restaurants would not serve blacks. To this day, I still dislike picnics.

5

Entrepreneurship and Public Service

Our parents were examples of how much could be achieved, given the rare opportunity to do so. Looking back over our lives, we were fortunate to have the love and support of our mother, father and extended family. But perhaps even more so, we were fortunate to experience first hand what it means to love one's "neighbor" and to care about that neighbor's well being.

The echoes still reverberate today in my mind—persons coming to our house, calling for mother. "Hattie!…Hat!….Miss Hattie!…Is she in?…Where can I find her?…I'll come back later," was a constant refrain. Indeed, Hattie Elizabeth Peters Clark seemed to be sought by everyone in the city. Whether real estate clients or strangers, people from every walk of life and background needed to see our mother about one thing or another, be it personal advice or help with business dealings. Thus, not only was our mother the center of our lives, she was the center of much of the community.

Mother was a suffragist of some renown in our state and ran for the state legislature. She and my father's commitment to end segregation in the public schools led to efforts at the state legislature to end the national practice. Lucille later sued the state of West Virginia for its discriminatory practices in the state's medical school admission. As a result, West Virginia paid for her and many other blacks to attend medical school outside the state. Mother also worked with unwed mothers in our town, a commitment in keeping with her social consciousness and dedication to helping the less fortunate in our community

The Great Depression of the 1930's did not directly affect our family, since around that time Mother made over $3,000 a month. While our family escaped the Depression, most other blacks, (and whites too, for that matter), in Charleston were not so lucky and joined the soup lines that snaked around the city blocks for miles on end. Our houses (the first one at 1690 Washington Street and the second, larger one at 1611 Washington Street) were often a haven for relatives and others coming to town until they were self-sufficient. The *inn* was never full. No one was turned away. A man named John Woods, who gathered trash in the neighborhood, lived with us until he found a place. He worked as our maintenance man. Our father insisted that we call him "Mr. Woods," even though it was common practice for children to address a laborer by his first name.

As the younger son, Charles was uniquely positioned in the family and mother both indulged him and taught him about her business dealings; things she did not teach the rest of us, at least not then. His natural interest made it all the easier for him to grasp the details of such grown-up activities as handling court cases and coordinating business deals in the town's law offices and banks.

As a lesson in discipline and hard work—lessons that would prove valuable in our lives in more ways than anyone could have predicted, each Clark child had to earn money in some way. We sold apples from the orchard our family owned in the country. Each summer, Charles and Carolyn sold pussy willows from the trees in our front yard. Charles also sold magazines and I sold the Evening Post at the capitol. I disliked selling so much that I hired another boy in the neighborhood to sell the apples for me.

6

College Years

When I entered West Virginia State in 1939, I found the coursework well within my intellectual grasp. I continued participating in track, so before I left West Virginia State, I honed my academic and athletic skills. As I neared the end of two years at West Virginia State, I looked for the school where I would complete my undergraduate degree. My love of track and the knowledge I had of Jesse Owens's extraordinary achievements at the 1936 Olympics in Germany influenced my decision to attend Ohio State, which I entered in 1941.

When Ohio State accepted me into its "hallowed halls of learning" I was not surprised, nor were my other family members. After all, attending West Virginia State had provided me with the confidence and the academic background to succeed. Ohio State University offered a broad-based, liberal arts education and a diverse range of study. I was among only a handful of blacks enrolled in the school. Since Ohio State had segregated living accommodations, I was not allowed to stay on campus, which did not help with my socialization. However, living off campus did give me plenty of time to study.

Experiencing integration for the first time, I was all too willing to show my classmates how capable I was academically, particularly in science and mathematics. Therefore, when I was the only person (in a class of 1,000) to make a perfect score on a chemistry test, I was very proud and told anyone who would listen that I had learned the fundamentals at West Virginia State. The day those results were posted, my usual loneliness was not nearly as overwhelming. What would my first grade teacher think of me now?

I continued my love for track and made the track team. Ohio State and other predominately white schools in the 1940's had a small sprinkling of black students on their sports teams. These students experienced the same prejudice as the race at large.

My two black teammates and I could not eat with the rest of the members of the team, nor could we order the same meals, due to what the coach claimed were budgetary constraints. However, during one such time, Bill Willis, (who later was inducted into numerous halls of fame), threatened that the coach would find himself getting up off the ground if the black teammates were not allowed to order what we wanted—namely a big juicy steak. Needless to say, justice reigned equal for all that day. Today, Willis is considered one of the greatest athletes ever to have played at Ohio State. He went on to a distinguished NFL career with the Cleveland Browns.

I continued to excel in track at Ohio State and became a varsity man. One year the school won a dual meet. In that competition, I won the high jump. The local newspaper ran a picture of some teammates and me in which I gestured with a fair amount of youthful optimism and confidence how high I would jump in the competition. Having proved I could compete with the best, the coach asked me to come back and run track as a graduate student. Having nothing else to prove to the school or to myself, I declined the offer with a great deal of satisfaction.

7

Medical School at Howard University

Our father's mantra was that each of his children should first learn how to get along with black people before learning to deal with whites. It was no accident that three of us were students at West Virginia State before transferring to other schools to graduate and later attended Howard University College of Medicine. Harriette and I attended the historically black state college before attending predominately white colleges (Smith and Ohio State, respectively), while Lucille transferred to Howard University. The three of us later attended Howard Medical School. Our experience at West Virginia State gave us extra self-confidence and more than an adequate educational foundation. Charles went directly to Howard out of high school (for undergraduate and medical school), as did Carolyn, who spent two years there before completing her undergraduate degree at Southern California University and returning to Howard for law school.

Lucille excelled in school. In elementary school, she won a prize for reading every book in the children's section of the library. A few years later, my younger sister, Harriette followed suit with the same accomplishment. Lucille's friends urged her to become a nurse, since she was excellent in science and math and had an interest in medicine. Our father, always the visionary, countered with, "Why not a doctor?" Our parents never placed a great distinction between the girls and boys. The girls were never told that they could not do something because of their gender.

The idea of becoming a doctor had not occurred to her before then, but it became Lucille's burning desire that stayed with her from college on. She attended West Virginia State from 1937 to 1939, and finished her undergraduate degree at Howard University in 1941. She finally realized her dream and obtained her medical degree from Howard in 1944. Lucille was one of only four women in her medical school class; however, the mostly male teachers and peers were quite supportive of Lucille and her female classmates. In fact, they did what they could to make her experience at Howard University both pleasant and successful.

For black students seeking a medical degree at Howard, including us Clarks, the traditions and rich legacy of the medical school were and still are a great source of pride. Its doors first opened in 1868, just three years after the Civil War ended, and just one year after the founding of the university in 1867. At that time, newly freed Blacks migrated in large numbers to the nation's capital. The college's founders recognized that an overwhelming number of Black people needed health care, and the only way to address the need was to train competent black men and women to go back to their rural communities and deliver desperately needed medical care. This fact was not lost on my father as he urged Lucille to become a doctor and encouraged Harriette, Charles and me in our pursuit of medical careers.

We all looked up to Lucille as a role model. When I arrived in 1943, I relied on her for an introduction to the social scene and advice on which courses to take. Lucille, who always felt responsible for her younger brothers and sisters, did not mind at all; she had promised Mother she would always look out for us, and to this day, she feels that same responsibility. Lucille helped me adjust to the rigors of medical school (it also helped that I had a photographic memory and did well in mathematics, chemistry and physics). During my long nights of study in medical school, I reminisced that the strict regimen of study through the summers and at 4 o'clock in the morning under the vigilant eye of my father was probably the best preparation I could possibly have had.

Fresh from Ohio State, I arrived at Howard University's medical school in June 1943. My dream of becoming a physician in order to help treat infectious diseases and decrease mortality and morbidity would be realized and Howard was the perfect place for the realization. Being the only person from Ohio State in my class, it was difficult at first to acclimate myself to the other students who had known each other for years as undergraduate students. Many were graduates of Howard, Lincoln, Morehouse and City University of New York (CUNY). My sister, Lucille and brother, Charles were already at Howard; Lucille, a junior in medical school and Charles, an undergraduate freshman. Their presence helped ease my transition from Ohio to Washington, D.C.

Despite not attending undergraduate with any of the kids in my class, I was elected class president for all four academic years. Since I certainly was not the most popular student, I believe my peers elected me because I was not afraid to voice my opinion. In medical school and throughout my professional career, I have been outspoken and opinionated, which resulted in my becoming a student leader with a reputation for militancy. During my tenure as president, I set up a tutoring system to help students experiencing academic difficulty. I also encouraged several members of the class to join me in taking the national boards instead of the state board exam. The national boards were more difficult and prestigious since they are recognized throughout the United States. We all did very well and completed the second series at the end of our internships.

At the end of my sophomore year, I was inducted into the honor society, Kappa Pi. At that time, honor societies were segregated and black students could not be inducted into Alpha Omega Alpha (which later merged with and replaced Kappa Pi).

When the number of Clark children attending the Howard University medical school reached four, my mother decided we needed a house. She eventually bought one for us at 69 Seaton Place, near Howard. Later we would purchase a property at 2570 Sherman Avenue, also near Howard University, where we would establish our medical practice, which is maintained to this day in our family.

Lucille graduated from the Howard University College of Medicine in December 1944. I graduated from the Howard University College of Medicine in 1946, succeeded by Charles in 1949 and Harriette in 1950. My youngest sister, Carolyn, always the individualist, graduated from the Howard University School of Law in 1953. She eventually left the law profession for her first love, children. She became a kindergarten teacher.

The next hurdle after finishing medical school was to decide which internship to choose. There were not too many choices in 1946. Due to segregation, our only choices were Freedmen's Hospital (later renamed Howard University Hospital), Harlem Hospital, Saint Philips Hospital, Hubbard Hospital and several small state hospitals. I was selected at all three of the major hospitals (Freedmen's, Harlem and Saint Philips). I elected to stay at Freedmen's since the obstetrics and gynecology department was fully accredited at that time.

At the completion of my internship, my course detoured for one year when the head of the OB/GYN department, Dr. Julian Ross, selected someone else for residency who was more conservative and less vocal than I. As a result, I spent the year of 1947-48, as an assistant clinical instructor in the Pathology department under Dr. Robert Jason, who later became Dean Jason. Due to what they deemed my outstanding qualities, Dr. Charles Drew, Dr. Frank Jones, and Dr. Paul Cornelly recommended me highly again to Dr. Ross for my residency. This time he accepted me.

8

Adelaide Friend Clark

I had renewed my friendship with Adelaide Friend while we both attended West Virginia State, where her parents worked. We first met when she was 12 years old at West Virginia's annual Golden Horseshoe history competition (which she won). Adelaide was keenly intelligent and she had a gift for remembering history. She later received her master's degree in business from Columbia University.

Adelaide and I married in 1946.

A naturally talented linguist, Adelaide was a true asset while we were stationed in Europe. Whether we were vacationing in France, Spain, Russia or Germany, she always served as translator.

For years, Adelaide worked as the assistant registrar at Howard University, where she was in charge of international graduate students. Adelaide was not only supportive of me while I was chairman of the obstetrics department; she was also committed to the success of the students, faculty, and school as a whole.

Aside from her work at Howard, she was a member of numerous charitable and social organizations, among them Alpha Kappa Alpha Sorority, The Links, Inc., The Pearls, The Girlfriends, and others too numerous to mention.

Adelaide died at age 73 from a cerebral aneurysm. The Washington Performing Arts Society, where Adelaide was an honorary member, created an endowment in her name to enable underprivileged children to experience the arts. A devoted wife and mother of our two sons, John III and Dwight Clinton, she was the symbol of beauty, grace, and class.

9

Practicing Medicine in the Military

Since there were so many students at Ohio State, the school had its own draft board, the Army Specialized Training Program (ASTP). During World War II, there was a blanket draft for which all men over 18 were eligible. The ASTP exempted medical students from the draft if they were physically fit (meeting army requirements) and if they were accepted into medical school (the Navy established a similar program).

Ohio State gave me three months to get into medical school before I would be drafted. My first choice was Ohio State. Because individuals (particularly black students) could not enroll in medical school unless they were Ohio residents, my father helped me secure residency. We decided to use my grandfather's address in Vinton, Ohio as my place of residence. Questioning my residency, Ohio State did not accept me into medical school. I was accepted later to several medical schools.

Now armed with the knowledge I was not accepted at Ohio State, my father busily set about getting me into the Howard University College of Medicine, where his friend Mordecai was president. While working on his master's degree at Harvard, my father met an impressive young man named Mordecai Wyatt Johnson who was studying to be a minister. He and Mordecai found they had common interests in many social causes pertaining to black people, and worked together on various projects during the summers. We played with Mordecai's children and grew very close to the Johnson family. Upon learning of my excellent academic record, President Johnson recommended immediate admission for me. On December 8, my birthday, Howard University telegraphed me, accepting me into the Howard University College of Medicine.

I entered medical school in June 1943 as part of the ASTP program. My ASTP medical school class was made up of soldiers (some civilians had trouble

21

meeting the physical requirements). The class consisted of 75 men and 4 women. Acceptance into the ASTP proved very advantageous for me. The program paid for my books, tuition and I received a stipend. Another benefit was the ASTP stimulated everyone to be successful in his or her studies. The army's rule was if you did not graduate on time, you would be transferred to a "quarter master unit" in Texas and would no longer be allowed to study medicine. In the first year, 10 individuals flunked out and left for Texas, though several of them finished medical school after the war.

When I was inducted into the Army in 1943, I was assigned to Fort Meade in Laurel, Maryland, in what was then a segregated Army. Blacks were not welcomed in the non-commissioned officers club and were assigned manual duties. Prejudice was rampant throughout the base. Fortunately, induction lasted only one week. Afterward, we returned to Howard to begin our study of medicine. The colonel in charge of us at Howard was not used to training doctors; he was used to training soldiers. He assigned us guard duty, imposed curfews, and required passes for travel. When the inspector general was informed of these actions, he reminded the colonel that it was more important that we be trained as good doctors for hospital availability, than learn military discipline.

Discrimination in the armed forces was the subject of widespread controversy. Blacks lobbied for equal treatment of black soldiers, including improvement in the living conditions that were woefully substandard to whites. For example, when newer eating facilities were built, blacks were relegated to the older, deteriorating facilities. More importantly, the army leadership perpetuated the belief during WWII that black people were not intelligent enough to serve in combat. Organizations like the NAACP and activists such as Charles Hamilton Houston (veteran of WWI, legal scholar, and dean of the Howard University Law School) argued for the complete integration of the armed forces.

On October 9, 1940, President Franklin D. Roosevelt issued a statement that the number of blacks inducted into the army should be in proportion to their population and that all combat and non-combat units, including aviation, would accept black soldiers. Officer Candidate School would be open to blacks, but graduates could serve only in black units where white officers would hold command positions.

My first military career ended June 1946, three years after it had begun. Academically, it was four years, because we recouped the last year of medical school by attending school all year without breaks. By graduation, the war had ended. I received the MD degree, plus a commission as a First Lieutenant. I was concerned about joining the reserves, since I preferred to continue my medical training. My dilemma was solved, as the Army did not want black medical officers in post-war occupied Europe. I was asked by letter to resign my commission, which I did, hastily.

In 1950, the Korean War erupted. Congress passed legislation to draft doctors since there was an acute need for medical officers. The doctors received financial assistance from the government and were eligible to be drafted for two years or more. By this time I had begun private practice and a little teaching. I received a telegram informing me I was in the Army as of 1952. My only choice was to volunteer as a captain or be drafted as a corporal. I chose captain, signed up, and shipped out to Texas for the physical training the Army required of doctors. After eight weeks of training in San Antonio, Texas, I was assigned to Europe.

The experience changed my mind about the military. I found that completely integrated armed forces made me more willing to fight and die for one's country. I was the first black doctor assigned to the 10th Field Hospital in Wurzburg, Germany, where there was a great need for obstetricians.

In Germany, I found the nurses and patients to be quite affable. I made many friends and became respected for my medical expertise. When the colonel's wife became ill, a white lieutenant under me from Amarillo, Texas requested my help with her diagnosis. He had warned her that it would be necessary to ask assistance from the "colored" doctor, Captain Clark. She replied that she did not care if I were green, as long as I could help. I was able to provide the needed assistance with the diagnosis and the colonel's wife and I established a friendship that existed throughout my stay. The white doctor whom I replaced had not been nearly as open. When I first arrived, he barely spoke to me and made no attempt to acquaint me with the city or with my responsibilities. As fate would have it, when I later became a department head in 1957 at Howard University Hospital, that same doctor applied for a position in my department. I did not hire him.

In 1952, I sent for my wife, Adelaide, and our son, John III. They traveled with me in Europe from 1952 through 1954.

When I was relieved from duty at the 10th Field Office, 400 people came to see us off. I was pleased to have served in the integrated army, and I gained a great deal of experience traveling through Europe as I evaluated local hospitals. Also, I was able to evaluate the European education system and to make a comparison between the civil rights and educational opportunities I found there with what was available in the United States. I was discharged in September 1954. Despite some negative experiences in the beginning, the station in Europe proved to be quite rewarding. The Army requested I re-enlist and become a major, but I had other goals to attain.

10

Making a Difference

When I returned from Germany in 1954, I accepted a position as clinical instructor at Howard University. From 1954 until 1957, I was a volunteer teacher at the medical school, since I had great interest in teaching. In 1956, I was promoted to assistant professor, then to associate professor in 1960 and finally to full professor in 1964.

In 1957, Dean Jason selected me to become the head of the department at 35 years of age (the youngest head of a clinical department at Howard University). If anyone had predicted this would happen only 11 years after my graduation from medical school, I would not have believed it. After all, I still considered myself (and was frequently reminded of the fact on the local social scene) not a Washingtonian, but a country boy from West Virginia. I had become an expert in my field and could now teach others, even though they were only a few years my junior. Of course, I met with some opposition from some of the older faculty members in my department who quite naturally wondered why they themselves were passed over for the cherished position of chair in favor of a younger, *less experienced* man.

At the time of my appointment, the OB/GYN department was under probation. I quickly worked with my staff and turned the department around. It was accredited throughout my tenure, which lasted until 1976.

The goals I set for the department were to train more minority doctors, to encourage students, and to foster relationships with local hospitals. I accomplished those goals by increasing the number of doctors in the department from 3 to 30. I encouraged the doctors to get specialized training beyond general OB/GYN, such as oncology, endocrinology, pre-natal effects on mothers, and public health. I invited outstanding guest lecturers to speak and to join the staff. I also encouraged my residents to write papers and participate in national meetings. I created a better relationship with Johns Hopkins, Georgetown, and George Washington University hospitals.

I fought many battles to secure residency for my students at some of the most prestigious universities in the nation. I also established affiliates at some of the local hospitals; D.C. General, Providence, and Cafritz. Those hospitals had mostly white patients, and they did not want young, black residents practicing their newly learned medical procedures on them. Such experimentation was reserved for black patients—poor, black patients. During my tenure as chair, residents gained experience by working for a short time in areas where black physicians' distribution was low for minority groups. These areas included Norfolk, Atlanta, New Orleans, Houston, and the Caribbean.

In 1974–1975, 100 percent of the students passed the Obstetrics and Gynecology Sections of the National Board Examinations and scored above the national average. In obstetrics, one student scored 755 and one student achieved 785 (the highest in the United States) out of a possible 800. The national norm was 512. Howard University's obstetrics-gynecology students scored on average 517. Also, during 1974, there were no maternal deaths at Howard University Hospital.

I am proud that we continue our effort to provide comprehensive screening tests for malignancies of the breast and female genitalia. The clinics continue to provide ambulatory services. The department remains committed to providing individualized care to every female who need obstetrical and gynecological consultation. In addition to routine clinics, Adolescent Gynecology, Fertility, Oncology, and Complicated Prenatal Clinics are in operation. The Oncology Clinic is equipped with a colposcope and cryosurgery unit.

An innovative and well-accepted service was the prenatal classes given to pregnant women and their spouses. The classes covered nutrition, healthcare, socioeconomic problems and personal awareness. Systematic instruction concerning the conduct and expectation of labor and delivery was also provided. Fathers-to-be were allowed to sit with their wives during labor and to witness the delivery of the baby. During the year 1974, 15,915 patients were seen in the Obstetrics and Gynecology Clinics. Plans were made to integrate these clinics with the Family Planning Clinics in order to fulfill the concept of total care.

During my quest to teach, I became head of the teaching department at Freedmen's, D.C. General, Cafritz, Norfolk General, and for four years at Providence Hospital. I realized in order to increase students' knowledge, it was necessary to publish in outstanding journals and to present lectures. Thus, I lectured throughout the United States and abroad in England, Russia, and China. To improve the health of our patients, we established a program with a large birth control clinic. A Pap smear grant allowed us to set up free Pap smear screening for students. We also extended training to students in the Caribbean, Puerto Rico, Hong Kong, and throughout Africa.

I did not run the department of Obstetrics and Gynecology alone. I am thankful for doctors and teachers like Ernest Hopkins, Lennox S. Westney, Alvin Robinson, Cyril Crocker, Collidge Gill, Olanrewaju M. Adeyiga, Horace Ward, Augustus O. Godette, Deborah Smith, John P. A. & Cosmos N. George, Francis Henderson, William Hill, Sydney Jones, Joseph Green, Phill Price. Slater Saul, Philip Turner, Richard Turner, Richard Blake, Richard Claytor, William Brown, Harry Martin, Cleveland Smith, Arvine Bradford, Patricia Schiller, Charles Cabiniss, Barbara Wesley, Clyde Freedmen, Robert Jason, Caryl Musended Ellis, William E. Hill, Elliese Smith, Sylvester Booker, Robert Greenfield, Robyn Arrington, D'Orsay D. Bryant, Ernest Cherrie, Wilbur Callender, Michael A. Jackson, Donald Sewell, Theodore George, James Willie, Joseph W. Isaac, Harold D. Johnson, Leroy Stiff, Ridgely Bennett, Dan Collins, Joseph T. Green, Bertram E. Stephens, Carol and Raymond Cutts, Tanner McMahon, Joseph Burke, James Gray, Michael Ivy, Peggy Scurry, Nixon Asomani, William Lofton, Jr., a special thanks to all of the deans that I served under as chairman: Robert Jason, Marion Mann, and K. Albert Harden, and a very special thanks to Anna Cherrie Epps and the ancillary staff at Howard, D.C. General, Providence, Norfolk General, and Cafritz Hospitals along with the preceptor hospitals in Houston, New Orleans, and Detroit.

The Clark sibling doctors at a medical convention in Washington, D.C. during the 1960's. From left to right: Drs. John, Lucille, Harriette, and Charles.

My wife, Adelaide, and I at the White House meeting with President Lyndon B. Johnson and Mrs. Johnson.

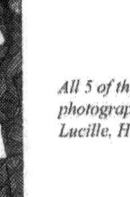

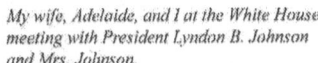

All 5 of the Clark siblings pose for a photograph. Left to right: Charles, Lucille, Harriette, Carolyn, and John, Jr.

Clark 1916 wedding announcement. John Sr. and Hattie on the steps after their wedding with various family members.

Shown in this 1916 photograph is the wedding party of JFJ Clark and Hattie Peters, the couple second from the left. Clark, who received his undergraduate degree from Chicago University and his master's from Harvard University, was the second principal of Garnet High School — from 1908 to 1946. As principal, he had the pleasure of handing a graduation certifi- cate to each of his five children. The Clarks had two sons, both physicians, and three daughters, two of whom also became physicians. The third daughter became a lawyer. Also seen in the photo, on the far right, is Byrd Prillerman, who was president of West Virginia State College from 1909 to 1919. The photo was submitted by Ferguson Meadows.

University of Chicago (1899) diploma awarded to John F.J. Clark, Sr.

A PROGRAM FOR
VOCATIONAL GUIDANCE IN GARNETT HIGH SCHOOL

By

JOHN FRANCIS JAMES CLARK

A Thesis Presented in Partial Fulfil-
ment of the Requirements for the Degree of
Master of Education in Harvard University

April 27, 1925

Patriarch (1925) John F.J. Clark, Sr's, Harvard University Masters Thesis on "Vocational Guidance in Garnett High School" where he served as principle for almost 40 years.

VOTE FOR

MRS. HATTIE E. CLARK

REPUBLICAN

HOUSE OF DELEGATES

Kanawha County

Your vote and influence appreciated

Lady from Tupper's Creek who made everything possible for the Clark family's success. Hattie Clark ran as a Republican for the Kanawha County, W.V. House of Delegates.

West Virginia State Capitol building.

John F.J. Clark at age 5.

Lucille, John, Harriette, and Charles.

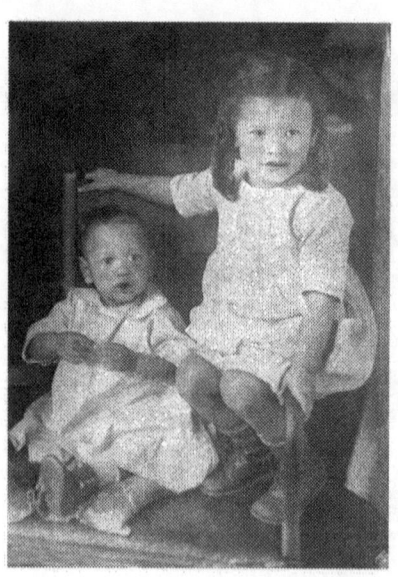

John and Lucille.

JESSE OWENS
1934-35 track
Then: One of the world's greatest athletes ever. The first American in the history of the Olympics to win four gold medals in a single games. At Ohio State, Owens was also dominating. He set three world records and tied a fourth at the 1935 Big Ten Championships. After his running days, Owens was a popular public speaker and sponsored youth sports programs all over the country.
Now: Owens passed away in 1980.

Garnet High School Graduation Class of 1939.

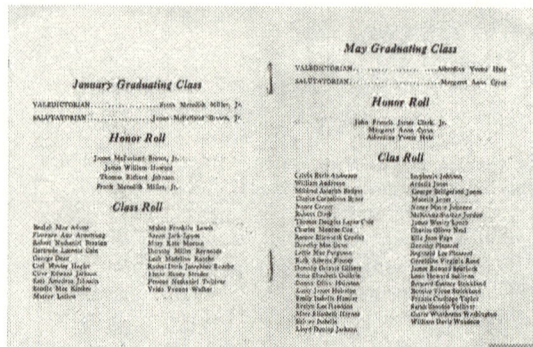

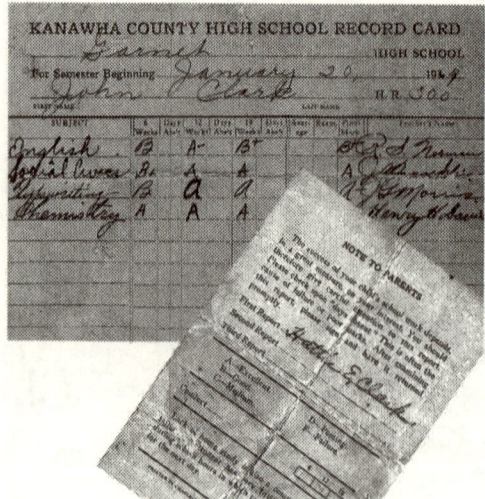

Despite battling dyslexia (unheard of at that time), John Jr. earns high marks his senior year at Garnet High School. (1939)

Ohio Varsity Track (1943) team photo with 3 African Americans members: Bottom row, second from the left: John F. J. Clark, Jr. (High Jumper and Long Jumer). Bottom row second from right: Chester Thomas (Sprinter), and Top row, forth from the left: William (Bill) Willas (Shot Put).

BILL WILLIS
1942-43-44 football
1942-43 track
Then: Considered one of the greatest athletes to ever play at Ohio State, Willis excelled at defensive middle guard on the football team. He was named All-American in 1943 and 1944. Went on to a distinguished career in the NFL with the Cleveland Browns.
Now: Belongs to numerous Hall of Fames, including Ohio high school, college, and pro football halls. One of the patriarchs of Buckeye football, Willis has stayed active with the program - dispensing his advice and wisdom to current student-athletes.

John F. J. Clark, Jr. (center) indicating how high he jumped in the track competition.

Dr. Mordecai W. Johnson to Speak

Dr. Mordecai W. Johnson, president of Howard University, Washington, D. C., will deliver the commencement address to the graduating class of Garnet High School, Thursday evening, May 27, in the school auditorium.

Graduating Medical School Clas from Howard Univerdity College of medicine (1946). The majority of the students were in the Army and graduated as first lieutenant and physician. Front and center: John F. J. Clark, Jr., who was president of his Medical School Class for all four achedemic years

My wife, Adelaide Friend Clark, visiting with Barbara Bush in the White House.

Family dinner with spouses, siblings, and children.

Citation

Adelaide Elizabeth Friend Clark
(Posthumously)
September 16, 1923 – August 27, 2007

Adelaide Elizabeth Friend Clark, is best remembered by the Howard University community as a devoted wife, mother, and humanitarian. Her interest in humanity was one of her greatest attributes. Indeed, her warm spirit and kind heart paved the way for a lifelong career dedicated to serving others.

Born on September 16, 1923 in Institute, West Virginia, Adelaide went on to earn the bachelor of arts degree from West Virginia State University, and the master's degree from Columbia University. Her early recognition of the value of education, not only from an academic perspective but from a people perspective, was shared by her husband and two sons, who have also dedicated their lives to serving others.

With all of her glamour, elegance, and grace, Adelaide committed her many talents and energy to helping the underserved, blossoming into one of Washington's most active and revered community leaders. She divided her time equally among a host of charitable and needy organizations including the Hospital for Sick Children, Children's Hospital, and the Mental Health Association of the District of Columbia. Howard University is especially grateful to Adelaide for her love and support of the Howard University Hospital. In addition to supporting her husband, Dr. John F. J. Clark, throughout his twenty-year tenure as chairman of the Department of Obstetrics and Gynecology, Adelaide was steadfast in her enduring commitment to raise monies for the University Hospital. Her efforts have indeed made an indelible mark on the entire University Community.

Throughout her life, Adelaide garnered tremendous recognition for her strong leadership roles in such groups as Friends of the Juvenile Court, the Women's Civic Guild, Jack & Jill, the NAACP, the Urban League, The Links, Inc., The Dolls, The Girl Friends, and Alpha Kappa Alpha Sorority. Her love of the arts also inspired many years of active membership on the Women's Committee and Board of Directors of the Washington Performing Arts Society, the Women's Committee of the National Symphony, the Friends of the Corcoran Gallery of Art, the Women's Committee of the Smithsonian Institution, the Washington Ballet, and the American Ballet Theater.

Adelaide Elizabeth Friend Clark, wife, mother, and humanitarian, was a woman of remarkable character and integrity. She was a selfless woman who willingly gave a piece of her heart to so many deserving people and causes. As a result of her efforts many have benefited, and for this, we are eternally grateful.

Howard University does now proudly confer upon Adelaide Elizabeth Friend Clark this citation of achievement.

Frank Savage
Chairman, Board of Trustees

H. Patrick Swygert
President

THE DISTRICT OF COLUMBIA

WALTER E. WASHINGTON
Mayor

WASHINGTON, D.C. 20004

October 4, 1977

John Francis James Clark, M.D.
4709 Blagden Avenue, N. W.
Washington, D. C. 20011

Dear Dr. Clark:

I am pleased to announce your appointment as a member
to the District of Columbia Commission on Licensure
to Practice the Healing Art for a term of three years,
to expire September 15, 1980.

I believe you will find your work with this Commission
to be a challenging and rewarding experience. You have
my personal best wishes for your willingness to serve
our community as a member of this Commission.

Enclosed are my Order No. 77-159, September 16, 1977,
announcing your appointment, and your Certificate of
Appointment.

With best wishes.

Sincerely yours,

Walter E. Washington
Mayor

11

Researching Maternal Health

Before I chronicle my research, I will provide a brief history of the beginning of maternal health care in the United States. After all, before black people began to address the need for maternal health care in their communities, the issue had long been advanced in the larger population, beginning with Mary Breckenridge in the early 1920's. This story cannot rightly begin without taking a brief look at the early days and research of maternal healthcare for women in general in the United States (unfortunately at a time when racism rendered maternal health care for black women and girls virtually nonexistent).

Until the 1930's, American women were more likely to die of childbirth than any illness, except tuberculosis. Women in rural areas were even more susceptible to the high mortality rate, particularly because hospitals and qualified medical care were almost non-existent in those parts of the country. As early as 1925, Mary Breckenridge, who established the first midwifery efforts, began her pioneering efforts to bring quality healthcare to rural America. During her travels through Europe following the end of WWI, she learned of midwifery. She decided to use her medical training to bring health care to mothers and children in rural America.

Later Breckenridge attended the Teachers' College of Columbia University, and the British Hospital for Mothers and Babies and the York Road General Lying in Hospital, both in London. Additionally, she traveled to Scotland to observe a community health care service staffed by nurse-midwives. By the time she established the Frontier Nursing Service at Wendover in Kentucky, she was not only a nurse, but also a trained midwife, certified by England's Central Midwives' Board.

In the years that followed WWI, the public expressed concern for the high maternal and infant mortality rates in the United States. The national maternal death rate was 6.7 per 1,000 live births (the highest in the western world), when she organized the frontier Nursing Service in 1923. Physicians, public health officials, and social reformers were also seeking solutions to the problem, and focusing on birth attendants, and supporting federal legislation in the form of Shepard-Towner Act, which attempted to support the education and training of midwives.

The Act authorized an annual appropriation of $1,240,000 for a five-year period, of which a sum not to exceed $50,000 was to be expended by the U.S. Children's Bureau for administrative purposes and for the investigation of maternal and infant mortality, the balance to be divided among the states accepting the Act as follows: $5,000 unmatched to each state, and an additional $5,000 to each state if matched, with the balance to be allocated among the several states on the basis of population and granted, if matched.

Breckenridge established Wendover (originally named the Kentucky Committee for Mothers and Babies) as a private, philanthropic organization, with the support of some of the most influential people in the state. For the next three years, Wendover functioned (in addition to being the administrative headquarters of the Frontier Nursing Service), as a cottage hospital. The nursing service was staffed by trained English nurse-midwives, along with Americans trained in England, as there was no U.S. training center at the time.

Although the emphasis was on mother and child, the nurses quickly became family nurses and Breckenridge and her nurses succeeded in providing quality maternity care. Nurse-midwives provided prenatal care and visited their patients bi-weekly until the seventh month and weekly thereafter. They handled dietary deficiencies and treated parasitic infections. The nurses were careful to maintain scrupulous aseptic conditions, despite the fact that most births took place within the patients' homes. Very rarely were invasive delivery procedures used; rather the nurses preferred natural delivery in the majority of cases.

During the Second World War, eleven of the already small number of nurses returned to England, leaving Wendover in a devastated condition. Recognizing the desperate need to replace the nurses, The Frontier Nursing Service gave rise to the Frontier Graduate School of Midwifery on November 1, 1939. With only two students in the first class, the first school of midwifery in the United States was born.

◆   ◆   ◆

When I began practicing medicine at Howard in 1954, the maternal health care of black women and girls, especially in urban areas, was very poor. During the next three decades I taught, conducted research, and collaborated with others in research into the causes of the high incidences of maternal death among this population. The articles and speeches I wrote or presented throughout my career fit two categories. The first is ectopic pregnancies (lectures throughout Europe, Russia and China). The second was on adolescent pregnancies (lecture mainly in the United States). Also, I was invited to testify before the Sub-committee on Fiscal and Governmental Affairs, Committee on the District of Columbia, U.S. House of Representatives in 1979 on the impact of teenage pregnancy.

As chair of the Department of Gynecology, I looked at a wide range of maternal death causes and maternal illnesses due to a number of factors, including hemorrhage, toxemia, and infection, and various forms of ectopic pregnancy (which are chronicled later in this chapter). From 1957 to 1968, my colleagues and I documented statistics from Freedmen's Hospital (Howard University Hospital) and the Iona Whipper Home, a domicile for pregnant girls in the Washington, D.C. area, supervised by the Department of Obstetrics and Gynecology at Howard University.

In addition to the high complication rate, poor prenatal care was paramount among these young mothers. Sixty-five percent did not receive prenatal care until the third trimester. Twenty-five percent received no prenatal care. In 3 studies of approximately 53 patients, the most outstanding complication of adolescent pregnancy was toxemia. With inadequate prenatal care, the incidence of toxemia increased significantly. Environmental control, coupled with good prenatal care, as provided at the Iona Whipper Home and by private physicians, helped decrease this serious complication.

My colleagues and I presented several social implications of this lack of prenatal care. We found teenaged pregnancy had reached epidemic proportions, particularly among the poor, the underprivileged, the uneducated, and economically deprived. It was predicted that the basic illnesses then affecting pregnant adolescents would continue to do so, if not corrected, and be perpetuated into the future. In regards to their infant births, increased retardation would result.

I also studied a group of 20 girls with normal to high IQs from underprivileged families whose incomes ranged from $3,200 to $5,200. The study showed these girls, when included in the normal education system, performed at levels of achievement that were equal, if not higher, than their counterparts with no experience with teenaged pregnancy. The study revealed, therefore, that a significant number of students with above average intelligence were dropping out of the school system due to teenaged pregnancy, with the long-term effect of diminished opportunities to reach their full potential educationally and the resultant effect of the likelihood of diminished educational achievement of their children.

My colleagues and I also documented the increased incidence of abortion. Specifically, changing sexual mores and liberalized social contacts between sexes had resulted in sexual experience at an earlier age. Unfortunately, according to our research, modern medicine did not progress at the same rate. Many in the adolescent group did not use contraception because they were uninformed and because they feared their parents would learn they were sexually active. This was particularly true of females, as they needed parental permission to get some types of contraceptives. Thus, abortion originated as a solution to the problem of unwanted pregnancy, according to our research.

It was my prediction, based on the high cost of hospitalization, the shortage of hospital beds, and the relative shortage of health manpower, that abortion would not be a satisfactory answer to the problem of an unwanted pregnancy, but that it would have a place in the total solution of the dilemma.

I also predicted a bleak future of a growing obstetric problem of toxemia and a growing trend in prematurity that also carried with it the risk of mental retardation. From the sociological standpoint, I showed that without specially designed educational programs, young women experiencing teenage pregnancy would become helpless and helpless dropouts of society. However, with special programs, they could be given some hope and expectation of better lives. I believed then as I believe now that this was definitely a disease of society, having its origins in the past, existing at that time, and without arrest and prevention, continuing to spread in the future.

A few years later, I documented a growing national trend in teenage pregnancy and presented data through my research that showed the social and medical implications. In 1960, for example the U.S. Vital Statistics indicated there were 4.2 million births, nationally. In 1967, the number of births was down to 3.5 million. This decline in the total number of births was in contrast with a sharp increase in the number of births among girls 16 years of age and under. In this group, the increase over the same 7 year period was approximately 36 percent. A number of factors were found to contribute to this increase, among them, the shift in the age distribution of the U.S. population. For example, the number of secondary school aged teens (14 to 17 years old) in the United States increased from 11.2 million in 1960 to 15.5 million in 1969. In 1960, of the 4.2 million births, 80,068 were to mothers 16 years of age or younger. Over this 7 year period, approximately a half million girls were school dropouts.

Ectopic Pregnancy

In 1959, Dr. Joseph Bourke and I documented in the American Journal of Obstetrics and Gynecology, one of the earlier source studies of ectopic pregnancies occurring in the Freedmen's Hospital from 1948 to 1957. We observed the number of ectopic pregnancies in the hospital was very high—1 in 84 pregnancies, as was the incidence of abdominal pregnancies—1 in 1,746 pregnancies. The clinical findings showed a relationship between pathogenesis of the abdominal pregnancies and the difficulty of diagnosis and surgical management.

Extra-Uterine Pregnancy

Studying the x-ray diagnosis of advanced extra-uterine pregnancy, (a pregnancy that is located outside the inner lining of the uterus) my colleagues, Drs. Javan Anderson, Sidney Jones, and I documented x-ray findings of 17 of 30 patients who had advanced extra-uterine pregnancies between 1946 and 1967. We concluded that exposing the pregnancy to radiological diagnosis was risky, but its benefit far outweighed the problem associated with extra uterine pregnancies.

Uteroabdominal Pregnancy

In 1961, Dr. Ridgely C. Bennett, who was also a doctor in the Department of Obstetrics and Gynecology at Howard University, and I conducted case studies in treating Uteroabdominal pregnancy. Uteroabdominal pregnancy is a form of ectopic pregnancy where a portion of the fetus is outside the uterus and a portion is within the uterine cavity—or a fistulous communication between the fetal membranes and eudiometrical cavity that would permit the passage of amniotic fluid or fetal appendages. The causes of this type of pregnancy were found to be (1) attempted criminal abortion; (2) defective scar (either from cesarean section or salpingectomy); (3) angular implantation of ovum; and (4) implantation of ovum in a stump of a tube. We found treatment of this type of pregnancy depended on a diagnosis that had to be differentiated from tubal pregnancies, fetal death en utero, threatened abortion, ovarian cyst, abdominal pregnancy, and in a congenital anomalous uterus.

Postpartum Complications

In the area of postpartum complications my research documented the incidence, severity, and end result of postpartum complications as a byproduct of many preceding factors. These included the interconceptional health status of the mother, antepartum care, intrapartum management, and multifactorial inputs during the aforementioned periods, which positively or negatively influence the well being of the mother and fetus. I found that the major alterations that occur are within the cardiovascular, pulmonary, hematopoietic, gastrointestinal, renal, muscumatopoietic, musculoskeletal, neurological, and psychological systems. Such complications included retained placenta, chronic villous invasion of the myometrium, lacerations of the perinea, vagina, cervix, vulva, perinea, and intra-abdominal hematomas, postpartum hemorrhage due to uterine mymetrial dysfunction, uterine rupture, uterine inversion, postpartum eclampsia, postpartum cardiovascular accidents, amniotic fluid infusion, pulmonary embolism, postpartum thrombophlebitis, cardiac arrest, puerperal infection, postpartum mastitis, complications of obstetric anesthesia, such as that associated with intravenous anesthesia, regional anesthesia, spinal anesthesia, general anesthesia, local anesthesia and post spinal headaches and current medicine.

Ectopic Pregnancy

I also made several observations in the area of ectopic pregnancy. First, I was appalled that the rate of maternal mortality in the United States among whites in 1963 was 24 out of 100,000 live births, while for non-whites it was 96 out of 100,000 live births. The causes were toxemia, hemorrhage, abortion, sepsis of pregnancy, and ectopic pregnancy. I found the improvement in maternal mortality was directly relational to the advent of antibiotics, perfection of blood storage and transition, improvement in diagnostic and treatment facilities, and public education.

However, the improvement in maternal mortality for non-whites had not kept pace with the improvement for whites. Specifically, ectopic pregnancy was still taking a significant number of lives. My colleagues and I found the newer textbooks were not discussing this type of pregnancy in a comprehensive manner. They were not discussing, for example, that these types of pregnancies were found to be the result of slow leakage of blood into the abdominal cavity, or tubal lumen, resulting in adhesions, walling off, and hematocele formation. As a result of the slow leakage, the complaints of the patients were spread over a long period of time. In a series of experiments, a palpable mass was the most serious findings in a chronic group. A mass was palpable in 37 percent of the chronic patients, and in only 22 percent of the acute patients. Abdominal tenderness was more prominent in the acute group, being present in 83 percent as opposed to 60 percent in the chronic group. There was little difference in the other signs. Cramp pain and spotting or bleeding, as was expected, had persisted for a longer period of time in the chronic group. We found that upon physical examination a subnormal or normal temperature should be suspect, especially in the patient of a working diagnosis or peltating complications.

Extra-Uterine Pregnancy

In 1987, Drs. Merceline Dahl-Regis, Roselyn Epps, and I reported findings from a study that included 45 advanced ectopic pregnancies from 1947 to 1984 delivered at Freedmen's Hospital and its successor, Howard University. Four patients of extra-uterine pregnancies were contacted to determine their developmental outcome. At the time of the study, their ages ranged from infancy to adulthood. Results were presented of two children who received in-depth interdisciplinary evaluations at the Howard University Child Developmental Center. My colleagues and I reviewed the literature and questioned other authors, who based on single examinations, reported normal functions in children born after extra-uterine pregnancies. In a long-term follow up study, we challenged then current research data and questioned earlier reports of the normal functioning of these same children. We concluded that each child should have the benefit of a total developmental assessment in all major categories at each stage from birth through adulthood

In 1984, I explored the fetal mortality rate from this condition, estimated at that time to be as high as 70 percent. I concluded this condition to be diagnosable through the following criteria; (1) vaginal bleeding accompanied by fetal heart irregularities; (2) vaginal blood determined to be of fetal origin; (3) palpation of vasoprevia through a dilated cervix; (4) visualization of vasoprevia through the anmioscope; and (5) marked fetal bradycardia when the membranes are unruptured and there is no evidence of vaginal bleeding.

I observed that the velamentous insertion of the umbilical cord is seldom diagnosed before a tragic accident occurs with the fetus and that survival rate is highest when a cesarean section is mistakenly performed for other causes. Also, I determined that the obstetrician should consider the possibility or an early sign of velamentous insertion of the umbilical cord if the membranes are intact and there is no evidence of vaginal bleeding.

Duodenal Atresia

Also, in 1984, I looked at the condition of duodenal atresia in the article, "Duodenal Atresia in Utero in Association with Down's Syndrome and Annular Pancreas" with Drs. Earle Hales, Peter Ma, and Samuel B. Rosen. We conducted research on a 28 weeks' gestational trisomic-21 (Down's syndrome) male with duodenal atresia due to annular pancreas, which is a ring or collar of pancreatic tissue that abnormally encircles the duodexium. The atresia was diagnosed in utero by sonographic techniques. In general, we concluded that prompt medical attention and surgical correction after high-resolution gray scale real-time ultra sounding imaging or fetal anatomy could salvage a condition that previously may have been fatal.

Causes of Maternal Mortality in the Late 20th Century and Early 21st Century

I still follow the research on maternal mortality and the health conditions that surround this issue. It is surprising to me that despite efforts to minimize the incidence of maternal mortality, conditions are almost as dire today as they were many years ago when I began to research the issue. For example, research shows that every minute of every day a woman dies as a result of pregnancy or childbirth, amounting to 500,000 annually in any given year worldwide. As it was 25 to 35 years ago, maternal death is still the result of many events that can occur in a woman's life, many of them non-medical. These events can be even more devastating in the lives of women living in economically deprived communities and in developing nations.

In a UNICEF publication titled, *The Lesser Child*, the disadvantages of being born a female are well documented. The publication states girls in developing countries are likely not to be breastfed and if they are breastfed, they are done so for shorter periods than boys. The result is they are malnourished from the beginning of their lives. They are subjected to heavy workload both inside and outside the home at an early age. When girls are ill they are less likely than boys to receive medical care. Among five-year-old girls, mortality exceeds that of boys by 20 percent in Bihar, Madhya Pradesh, Manipur, Punjab, Rajasthan, Tamil Nadu, and Uttar Pradesh in India.

In his publication, *The State of the World's Children*, Grant has shown the relationship between the female literacy rate, contraceptive prevalence, the Crude Birth Rate (CBR), and the maternal mortality rate. For example, in Bangladesh, the female literacy rate is 19 percent, contraceptive prevalence is 25 percent, the CBR is 41 percent, and maternal mortality is 600 per 100,000 births. In India, the female literacy rate is 29 percent, the contraceptive prevalence is 34 percent, the CBR is 31 percent and maternal mortality is 340 per 100,000 births. In Malaysia, the female literacy rate is 65 percent, the contraceptive prevalence is 54 percent, the CBR is 32 percent and maternal mortality is 59 per 100,000 births. On the other hand, Singapore has a female literacy rate greater than 80 percent, a contraceptive prevalence of 74 percent; the CBR is 18 percent and maternal mortality is 5 percent.

Sex determination by Chronic Villus Sampling (CVS), although illegal, continues to be practiced in countries where the desire to procreate a male child is great and deeply embedded in tradition. This entire subject is related to several closely knit diehard practices, including the reluctance to and difficulty of educating female children, much less the anxiety of providing a dowry. The anxiety of saving hard earned money for a dowry and even, after marriage, the constant and repeated demands from the family of the groom are hard to meet. "Dowry deaths" still continue as do the physical and mental torture of young girls. Research also shows the very old practice of female infanticide continues and the rate of suicide and homicide among women and girls continues at alarming rates.

Additionally, the Indian Institute of Management conducted a study that found the ratio of men to women seeking medical attention at a primary health center was 5:1. Because of ignorance and household responsibility, women neglect themselves.

Despite the enormity of the crisis worldwide, maternal deaths due to hemorrhage, infection, toxemia, and cardiac disease are declining in the West due to improved medical practices. Cardiac disease during pregnancy is associated with a high mortality. Heart disease can be congenital, but most likely it is acquired. It is the aftermath of inadequate treatment of childhood rheumatic fever. Valvular disease of the heart follows, which jeopardizes the life of the young girl when she is pregnant. Similarly, acute nephritis following a sore throat can lead to nephropathy and chronic hypertension. When patients with chronic hypertension are pregnant, they are prone to super added toxemia with all its serious consequences. In the U.S., ectopic gestation is still one of the leading causes of maternal death.

In reference to abortion, 150,000–200,000 deaths occur worldwide from abortion annually. Of the maternal deaths in South America, close to 50 percent are due to abortion.

Although tetanus toxoid is freely available; according to a study conducted by the London School of Hygiene and Tropical Medicine, 15,000–30,000 cases of maternal tetanus occur annually—a neglected cause of maternal mortality.

Research shows AIDS to be nearly epidemic in certain countries, revealing a need for all women to be tested and counseled routinely for HIV. In this scenario, health officials would prevent HIV infection in women of childbearing age, prevent pregnancy in HIV-infected women, and interrupt the vertical transmission of infection from an infected mother to her child.

Important contributing causes of maternal mortality in developing countries are anemia, poverty, ignorance and malnutrition, repeated pregnancies, inter current infections, parasitic and helminthic infestations, and haemoglobinopathies. The percentage distribution of deaths from puerperal sepsis was 13.1 in 1986. Research shows it has been reduced to 8.1 in 1990.

During my career, my lectures and other professional activities took me across the United States and beyond to many other countries, including Jamaica, Bahamas, Haiti, Puerto Rico, Grenada, Virgin Islands, Trinidad, Guyana, and Bermuda. In Africa, I traveled to Cameroon, Ghana, Liberia, Uganda, and Nigeria, and in Asia to Hong Kong.

During the ensuing years, I devoted my career to providing proficient medical care for women and children. I delivered more than 7,000 babies. I was also editorial consultant for the Journal of American College of Obstetricians and Gynecologists.

12

The Prophecy Fulfilled

Father was convinced education was the salvation for the descendants of Africa in America. He believed that only after three successive generations could families break free of the constraints of race and the history and deprivation of slavery. There could be no generation that skips education and economic achievement without the family having to start over again. During his lifetime, even as he fought tirelessly for the social and economic development of the black community of West Virginia, my father sought to lay the foundation for the fulfillment of his prophecy within his own family. If Father were alive today, he would see that his prophecy has been more than fulfilled. Three successive generations have now broken the iron grip of slavery.

As if somehow prophetically predestined, my grandmother Lucy began to break the chain even before my father's birth by enrolling in Oberlin College in 1872. In the next generation, my father graduated from the University of Chicago and Harvard University; and in the third generation, my brother, sisters and I graduated from Howard University's Medical and Law schools. Even beyond my father's original vision, his great, great, great grandchildren—the fourth and fifth generations—continue to fulfill the vision of his prophetic words spoken almost one hundred years ago.

During her medical career, my sister, Lucille, worked in public health at the New York University and as a physician in the Unified School District in Los Angeles for 30 years. Lucille's husband was Paul Lawrence "Tank" Younger, who was the first national football player to come from a historically all-black college (Grambling State University) and he was the first black player to play in an NFL All-Star game. After his career as a player, he went on to become the League's first Black assistant general manager. Paul Younger was elected to the College Football Hall of Fame in August 2000.

Lucille's children are Howard Clark Lewis, who received his B.S. in business management from the University of Southern California, and is currently a vice president with City National Bank in Torrance, California; Harriette Elizabeth Lewis, who received a B.S. degree from the University of California at Berkeley and an M.D. degree from Morehouse Medical School and is currently an emergency physician at Daniel Freeman Hospital in Inglewood, Calif.; Lucy Younger, who received a B.A. degree from the University of California at San Diego and an M.L.A. degree from the University of California's Berkeley College of Environmental Design. She is currently a project manager with Los Angeles County. Lucille has one grandchild, Andrew David Lewis.

Also, following in the Clark tradition and fulfilling the prophecy, my older son, John Francis James Clark, III is an obstetrician/gynecologist and teacher. A graduate of Meharry University Medical School, he is an assistant clinical professor at Colombia University Medical School. His wife, Marva Mitchell Clark, is the chief of staff for a large dental group. The oldest of his children John IV, has entered the world of finance and economics by studying business at Florida A &M University. John III and his wife Marva have two children Kyle and Zoë.

My younger son, Dwight Clinton, completed his undergraduate degree at Howard University. He later earned an M.B.A. and has worked almost exclusively in the healthcare field, designing and organizing health programs. His wife, Vanessa Washington Clark, is a senior systems analyst. They have one child, Nicole Renée, who attends Trinity College.

My brother, Charles, unlike Lucille and me, went directly to Howard University at the age of 16 in 1943, after winning a competitive scholarship for which he ranked second in the region. After completing his undergraduate work at an accelerated rate of two years, he continued his education at Howard University's medical school. His love and natural talent for subjects such as anatomy and physiology led him to become a surgeon. During his career, Charles was the senior resident and chief resident in Surgery at Freedmen's Hospital, which was later remodeled and renamed the Howard University Hospital. Charles was also a fellow of the American Cancer Society and the assistant chief of surgery at the Veteran's Administration Hospital in Tuskegee, Alabama. During his tour of duty with the Navy, Charles traveled throughout the world. Yet, Charles considers his greatest accomplishment to be the 40 years he taught at the Howard University Medical School, where he was an associate professor. Charles maintained a private practice as a surgeon for many years.

During his residency, Charles married Jeannine Smith, a Howard alumna. Jeannine earned a degree in German and English. She later returned to Howard to earn a master's in African Studies. After raising their three children, Jeannine went on to hold various posts in the arts, including a position on the Board of Regents at the Smithsonian Institution.

Charles and Jeannine have three children: Charles H. and Jeannine (twins) and John Elliot. Charles, Jr. received his undergraduate degree from Amherst College and his medical degree from Howard. He works in public health with a specialty in addiction medicine. Jeannine graduated from Georgetown Medical School and now practices as a pediatrician. John Elliot also attended Amherst College, where he earned his bachelor's degree. A graduate of George Washington Medical School, he is a surgeon. Charles and Jeannine have six grandchildren, Christopher Clark Jeffries, Angelica Noel Clark, Kelly Marisa Clark, Dana Jeannine Clark, Sydney Amelia Clark, and Scarlett Olivia Clark.

My sister, Harriette, who attended Smith after her two years at West Virginia, graduated from Howard University Medical School in 1950. While at Smith, as one of only six black students in the school, she excelled in her pre-med courses and in her laboratory assignments. Our parents paid for a single room so she would not have to endure the racism that may have dampened her experience in the elegant living quarters of the large gracious houses that served as dormitories in those days. Harriette was the only girl of color in the class of 1946. Harriette was married three times (all of her husbands are deceased).

Harriette has two sons: Cleveland Robert Chambliss, Jr., a graduate of the Morehouse School of Medicine, and Marque Clark Chambliss, a graduate of Harvard University and the Boalt Hall School of Law at Berkeley. She has two grandsons, Robert III and Ryan.

My sister, Carolyn Clark Smith spent two years at Howard University. She received her bachelor's degree from the University of California at Los Angeles, her law degree from Howard, and her teaching credential from the California State University. She was an elementary school teacher for the Los Angeles Unified School District for 20 years. Her husband, Frank Lloyd Smith, currently retired in Las Vegas, was a sales representative for National Distilleries for 25 years. Their children are Carole Clark McCants, who received her bachelor's degree from Mills College in Oakland; Beverly Lynn Clark, a graduate in political science from Pepperdine; Greta Smith Garcia, who received a bachelor's degree in English as a Second Language from California State University; and Stephen Monroe Smith, who received his bachelor's degree in biology from Stanford and his medical doctor degree from Howard University. Carolyn's four grandchildren are Amy Arlene Carolyn McCants, Clark Calvin Ryan McCants, Garrick Joaquin William Garcia, and Stephen Smith.

Carolyn died in a tragic car accident in 1978 at the age of 49.

13

Closing Letters

As I reflected upon more than sixty years of friendship, I have been amazed by the events that were triggered by our meeting in 1938 at the American Legion's First Boys State for young men of color at West Virginia State College. As I recall, the objective of the Boys State was to expose young men to the organization and functioning of state government. Consistent with established public policy there was a separate Boys State for white young men as well.

You and I became friends when I agreed to serve as your campaign manager following your decision to run for the office of governor. As I recall, young men of high school age came from all over the state. We won the election with a flourish and you assumed your position of leadership. In connection with my service as your campaign manager I was called upon to make a speech outlining your "promises" and commending you to the delegates to the Boys State. President John W. Davis of West Virginia State College was standing in the rear and heard the speech. Later he initiated a conversation with me which resulted in my matriculation at the College and that was a critical decision which resulted in many positive events in my life.

I was delighted when I learned that you were going to be my roommate when you entered West Virginia State in 1939. We roomed together for two years in Prillerman Hall. I remember being impressed by the fact that I would be rooming with the son of the Principle of Garnet High School in Charleston. Your father, J.F.J. Clark, was a noted and highly respected person in educational and community circles in the State. You and I hit it off immediately. We shared the same values, i.e., commitment to high academic performance, responsible social relationships, intellectual and academic interests, and respect for property and rights of other students. I do not recall that we ever had a serious disagreement in our time as "roomies." I know how much I regretted your transferring to Ohio State University at the end of your sophomore year.

I can recall images of you studying at your desk. I never saw a person who demonstrated more intensity and purpose than you did. I tried to respect your space and academic efforts, though I was sometimes amused by comments you made about various teachers and the demands they were placing on you. I was not surprised that you entered medical school and became the highly respected physician-surgeon you are after your graduation.

I had become a "sphinxman" in Alpha Phi Alpha in spring semester of 1939 and was initiated into the fraternity in the fall semester of the same year. I was glad when you decided to pledge in Alpha in the spring of 1940 and participated in your initiation in the fall of 1941. Your initiation and the one preceding it caused me to determine that the "paddling" was excessive and resulted the next year in a severe restructuring of the initiation process.

Over the years our paths crossed only infrequently, but I was glad to rekindle our friendship when I took up residence in Washington in the summer of 1975. I never fail to enjoy being in your company and listening to you commend your opinions and convictions in conversation. I sometimes wonder what became of the quiet young man with whom I roomed in college. Knowing you has been one of the treasured relationships in my life. I am looking forward to the publication of your life story. I know that it will be rich and filled with wisdom. I treasure our friendship and wish you good health, long life, and the fulfillment of your most cherished dreams

Lawrence N. Jones
Dean Emeritus of the School of Theology
Howard University

John and I met in the late summer of 1943 at Howard University College of Medicine. We were freshmen, 2 of 76, mostly men, from all over the country.

We were very serious young people because our nation was at war. We began our life as medical students approximately one and one half years after President Roosevelt asked for and received from Congress, a Declaration of War following the Japanese bombing of Hickham Air Force Base at Pearl Harbor. Now our enemies included Japan, Germany, and Italy, and we were aware of the importance of our education; that it was imperative that we learn how to be good doctors, and therefore quite necessary that we pass our courses.

We were 76 strangers. No one really knew anyone else in the class. It was immediately evident that John was perhaps the most extroverted and out-going member of the class. His open friendliness encouraged feelings of confidence and comfort in all of us during this scary period when news of the War was all around us. John seemed at ease with everyone. He even conversed freely though always courteously with our teachers.

I soon learned that he was a proud graduate of Ohio State University. John was a bright student and well prepared academically to study medicine.

Because of his popularity the class elected him president. Soon John knew much about all of his classmates, who they were and where they came from, and had become genuinely involved in their problems. He proved himself to be a true and unusual leader, always keeping the class on a steady and increasingly self-confident course. It seemed that all of John's classmates loved and respected him for his sense of humor and likeable personality, and were happy to be in his company.

After graduation when the members of the class went their various ways, John kept in touch in spite of a challenging schedule. Kitty Roett, who had served as our class secretary, returned to Texas to practice, bequeathing her position to me, since it was assumed that having served during school years as assistant secretary, I possessed the necessary skills. Beside, I was on hand, since John and I lived in the same city, and for many years shared a neighborhood. Often he would ask me to make a phone call or to send a letter to a former classmate. At all times he knew the whereabouts and condition of every classmate. He made sure that every classmate received a special invitation to attend class reunions. Classmates came, if they could, to participate in the University activities. But what really drew them I think, were the class get-togethers that we in the area joyfully planned, inspired by his enthusiasm. Such continuing concern for his classmates indicated to me that he grew up in a strong and family oriented home.

John continued to grow professionally, becoming an outstanding obstetrician and gynecologist, who while still a young man assumed the Chair of the Department of Ob-Gyn at Howard. In his role as head of the Department, he instructed and inspired many students, residents, and nurses.

Today, John and I are the two members of the Medical Class of '46 who remain in the Washington area. We see each other infrequently. However, the high regard and love I developed for him while we were students remains constant. He is still bright and witty, and most importantly, remains my good friend.

Wilber F. Jackson, M.D.

To see one of our own become the professor and the chairman of the department was a proud moment for the staff; your classmates, and alumni. Your leadership as the professor and chairman was defined by significant events that raised the department's standards to another level. Your creative teaching techniques, methods and programs for the students prepared them to perform well on State Board exams.

The trained black Ob-Gyn specialists from your program numbered more than any institution in the country. They all became certified by the specialty boards and are giving service throughout the United States and some foreign countries. You brought national exposure to our department my giving lectures at various meetings around the country and inviting distinguished professors from other medical schools to give seminars at Howard University.

In 1981, the College of Ob&Gyn sponsored a series of lectures with Harvard University in Communist China. You were one of the lecturers. Your paper was well received especially when you gave it in Chinese. Dr. Tanner McMahon and I were with you in attendance. You were well received in Berlin in 1984 at the World Congress of OB&GYN. We met several of your trainees at that meeting. Those meetings gave the department international exposure.

Your tenure as the professor and chairman of the Department of OB&GYN in my view, and without hyperbole, was outstanding.

Alvin F. Robinson, M.D.

It is a distinct pleasure for me to write a letter about my colleague and friend Dr. John F. J. Clark. I first met him when I was a third year medical student and he was Chief Resident in Obstetrics and Gynecology (OB-GYN) under Dr. Julian Waldo Ross—the longtime professor of OB-GYN at Howard. As students, we all really wanted to make rounds with John Clark because he was said to be "really heavy" (that is, he knew everything that was worth knowing about OB-GYN). We were not disappointed.

When I returned to the surgical faculty in 1962, John was professor and chairman of the department of OB-GYN. When I became chairman of our department in 1970 (a position I held for 25 years), I had several long conversations with John, not only because his students had the best performance on the National Board of any of the clinical disciplines, but also because almost all of his residents were passing the specialty Board on their first attempt. He told me of his firm commitment to Howard and to the young men and women who were medical students and residents. He said it was his obligation to give them his best and to inspire them to strive for excellence.

However, there is one episode that had a profound impression on me that let me know the kind of man he really was. There was a young medical student who developed a malignant GI tumor on whom I operated twice. Time subsequently proved to us that he had been cured. This young man had a great desire to obtain a residency in OB-GYN. I spoke to John on this man's behalf (John, you know it was George Sherman). He told me that several of his faculty told him not to accept Sherman as a resident because it was likely that he would develop a cancer recurrence and not be able to complete the residency. A few days later, George Sherman was in my office with a big smile on his face stating that he had been chosen for one of the highly sought positions in the OB-GYN residency. Naturally, I was very happy for him. I then went to John to thank him for going against the wishes of departmental faculty to take this young man into the OB-GYN program, who not only completed his residency, but developed a highly successful practice in his hometown. He is still active in practice there. John told me that he knew if this man was unable to complete the residency, some departmental faculty members would tell him what a great mistake he had made. He then added, "But in my heart I know that I made the right decision. It's not often that as one individual you have the opportunity to make a decision that can have a profound impact on someone's life. But when you have that opportunity and you believe that it is the right thing to do, you should do it." Of course, things worked out well and John's decision was the correct one. Even if the young man had not been able to complete the residency, I believe that John had made the right decision.

I think you can understand why this episode more than any other let me know the real John Clark, what he was really all about—his inner self. I have the highest personal and professional regard for John Clark for the reasons I have given above.

LaSalle D. Leffall, Jr., M.D., F.A.C.S.
Charles R. Drew Professor of Surgery

John F.J. Clark Jr., M.D. to me can only be described as, "A Giant of a Man and a Man for All Seasons."

To me he exemplified the epitome of leader, teacher, and physician and demonstrated paternal qualities that made me feel honored and proud that I was chosen by him to be a resident under his tutelage.

As a teacher, he had the ability to make the most complex of problems simple, the most difficult of cases easy, and the most laborious of tasks enjoyable.

As a leader, he set excellent examples to follow, and instilled in me a sense of pride and patience that demonstrated it was prudent to persevere and that success always came to those with patience and endurance.

His paternal instincts gave me a sense of belonging and made me feel like a sibling in his extended family of the department. He was, and still is truly a man for all seasons.

Dr. Clark is and has been the most influential man in molding my life, both as a person and as a physician. He has influenced the direction of my life, the quality of my life, and the ambitions and success of my life. He has truly been a role model for me.

George H. Sherman, MD, FACS, FACOG
Consultant Chief Emeritus-Ob/Gyn
The Princess Margaret Hospital
Nassau, Bahamas

I first met Dr. John Clark during the winter of 1959, which was the second semester of my sophomore year at Howard University College of Medicine. He was chairman of the department of obstetrics and gynecology and his reputation had preceded his first lecture. Most of my classmates had heard of his devotion to teaching and excellence, and greatly anticipated his first lecture. It was during this exposure that I developed an interest in obstetrics and gynecology that was consummated during the clinical rotation of my junior year.

During that rotation, I had the opportunity to observe and learn from the most respected obstetrician in the Washington, D.C. area. It appeared we had at least one delivery a day that gave the medical students, interns, and residents ample exposure to his obstetrical philosophy. His respect for and devotion to his patients was contagious, and I began to imagine how great it would be to "grow up" and be like the "Chief."

Following the completion of my junior year and after my clinical rotation in obstetrics, Dr. Clark selected me and another classmate to be externs in obstetrics at D.C. General Hospital for the summer. We knew the political and educational ramifications associated, since we were the first junior medical students from Howard University to train in this arena. Our dedication and representation were outstanding, and I am sure that he made a great selection. Our knowledge and clinical experience led to immediate acceptance by the residents, interns, and senior students from Georgetown and George Washington Universities.

After my senior rotation in obstetrics and gynecology at D.C. General Hospital and after my rotating internship at Freedmen's Hospital, Dr. Clark selected four first year residents, and sent me and another first year resident to D.C. General for our first year of training.

During these first years of Howard's association with obstetrics and gynecology at D.C. General Hospital, we were not welcomed with opened arms by the Ob-Gyn departments of Georgetown and George Washington Universities. Dr. Clark did a tremendous job in leadership and his insights and commitment were responsible for developing D.C. General into an excellent training institution for Howard University. During this same period, he developed an affiliation with Norfolk Community Hospital that allowed his residents an abundance of clinical training.

He encouraged excellence. All of us thought of ourselves as superior surgeons. Because none of us has ever failed board certification, each of us was motivated not to be the first failure, and this success continued for many years.

Dr. Clark knew from experience what we needed during training to become outstanding clinicians and exposed us to the required and necessary training. His obstetrical and gynecological philosophy provided me with a base and guided me during 28 years of private practice. No other professor has been a greater influence on me than he has.

He is a living legend who has demonstrated integrity, intelligence, teamwork, organizational skills, community commitment, humor, and the ability to teach and communicate. His residents were well trained to practice obstetrics and gynecology. He has trained more black obstetricians and gynecologists than has any other person. All of us will forever be indebted to him for his leadership and for our excellent training.

Dr. Clark, I thank you for the guidance, advice, training, and concern that you have given me through the years. Thank you so much for accepting me as a resident and for influencing many of my past choices. You are the ultimate professional, and I will always be grateful for the association.

Horace Ward, Jr. M.D.

It is with the deepest appreciation that I write you this letter. I believe in giving people roses while they can still smell them. That is why I'm writing this letter to let you know what a profound effect you had on my career.

When I came to the Howard University College of Medicine, I did not know in what I wanted to Specialize. I quickly found out that I liked the Operating Room but I still did not know what branch of Surgery to pursue. Then I had the opportunity to rotate through Obstetrics and Gynecology under you, Dr. Clark. I immediately appreciated the warmth and closeness of the department members and the strong leadership of "The Chief." Then I found out that "The Chief" was from my home state of West Virginia. About the same time you, Dr. Clark, found out that I was from West Virginia and the bond was set. You constantly pushed me towards excellence "to hold up West Virginia." It was just the inspiration I needed to keep on keeping on. I was a mother trying to raise a child while completing medical school and sometimes things got pretty rough. However, I felt I had to push to excel because I just couldn't let you down. As I rotated through Obstetrics and Gynecology, I realized that I had found my niche. I could do surgery and get the bonus of delivering babies—something I always felt was next to miraculous.

Dr. Clark, you taught me so much about science, but more importantly, the art of Medicine. You made me understand that we were not treating "cases." We were treating people who happened to be sick or in need of medical care. When patients were sometimes less than ideal, you made me look through the dirt and grime or obesity or drunkenness and see a person in need of help. I'll always remember you saying to us, when we were shying away from operating on an obese lady that fat people don't want to be sick either. These lessons have stayed with me throughout my life. I remember you telling us that when a patient comes to us, be grateful. After all, they had to pass by approximately 20 other qualified gynecologist to get to us. You taught us never to take a patient for granted and treat every patient as we would want our own family treated.

While teaching us these lessons, you also taught us not to think too highly of ourselves. You wanted to remind us that we were not gods. But with the right attitude, we could be God's instruments. You chastised us when needed but never maliciously. We always knew you were trying to make us the best we could be. You taught us how important it is sometimes just to listen. You taught us to never be ashamed to ask for help or get a second opinion. You taught us the importance of looking out for each other and watching each other's backs.

Dr. Clark, I truly feel that the Department of Obstetrics and Gynecology has never been the same since you had to step down because of illness. I hope that in the near future there will rise up another great leader to restore the department to its former state of excellence. In the meantime, just know that the majority of Black Obstetricians and Gynecologist have you to thank for their training and ultimate success. I thank God every day that I had the opportunity to train under you.

Elliece S. Smith, M.D.

As a medical officer at the U.S. Food and Drug Administration, I enjoyed working with you on many occasions when you were selected by your peers to serve as consultant to the Obstetrics and Gynecology Advisory Committee of the U.S. Food and Drug Administration. You always demonstrated unusual clarity of thought and facility of expression. Your contribution to the regulation of drugs for use in obstetrics, gynecology, and family planning resulted in the provision of high quality reproductive health care to American women.

Ridgely Bennett
Former Medical Officer
Food and Drug Administration

Dr. Clark, I met you in 1962, I was a freshman medical student whose wife was pregnant, and we came to you for prenatal care and delivery. My son, Charles, was born June 15, 1963. During Pharmacology in my sophomore year, I was sent to the operating room at Freedmen's Hospital to view the use of anesthetic agents. The operation I saw was a cesarean section performed by you. I was awe-struck. Upon getting the go-ahead by the anesthesiologist, it seems there was a blur of motion, a flash of steel, a spurt of blood, and then...a baby. It was the most dramatic event I had ever seen and for the time, I was hooked. I thoroughly enjoyed my Ob-Gyn clerkship, but as much as I enjoyed obstetrics, I found gynecology problematic. Perhaps it had to do with the illegal abortions, which we faced at that time. My choice of internal medicine as a specialty and gastroenterology as a subspecialty had more to do with the comprehensive appeal of that discipline to me than anything else.

Nevertheless, you always stood out for me as the complete role model, as a physician, teacher, and more importantly, as a kind human being. When I became a faculty member, you were still close by. You were always free with your support and advice, for which I will also be eternally grateful.

For so many years, you were the primary educator of African-Americans in their preparation to become specialists in obstetrics and gynecology in the United States, and you have been acknowledged in so many forums for this very significant contribution.

Therefore for many reasons, I feel uniquely qualified to attest to the value of your career to the country, the community, to Howard University, to the Department of Obstetrics and Gynecology, and to myself. We can all look back at some point and find some situation we wish we had handled differently, or wish we could have back. If you have such memories, be very sure that they are very miniscule compared to the wealth of good that you have accomplished.

Victor F. Scott, M.D.
Vice President of Medical Affairs
Howard University College of Medicine

Congratulations on your memoirs. Yours is an inspiring and interesting story and one that should be recorded. We have known you as a friend and medical colleague for almost 50 years.

You were an officer in the Army Medical Corps the first time we saw you, when you visited Dr. Julian Waldo Ross at Freedmen's Hospital. Our class of medical students learned that you were destined to become a faculty member when you left the Armed Services. You joined the Obstetrics and Gynecology faculty in 1956 during our internship and we regarded you as bright, competent and compassionate instructor from whom we learned a lot.

At the young age of 35 years, you succeeded Dr. Ross and became the Chairman of the Department in 1957. As Program Director from 1957 to 1976, you trained more African American OB-GYN specialists than anyone else in the world. While you were fulfilling the demands of an enormously busy professional career, you made time to be a forceful advocate for the citizens of the District of Columbia and you have given effective testimony before government agencies on many occasions.

During your career, you have received numerous awards from all sectors of our profession. In 1976, you were awarded the William Alonza Warfield Award by the Association of Former Interns and Residents of Howard University Hospital and the Outstanding Teacher award by the Student Council of the College of Medicine. In 1978, you received the Kaiser Permanente Award for Excellence in Teaching from the College of Medicine and the Outstanding Clinical Instructor Award from Howard University Hospital. The Medical Society of the District of Columbia awarded you the community Service Award in 1985. In 1994, you were named Distinguished Physician, Teacher and Scholar by the National Medical Association. We felt honored to participate in the establishment of the John F.J. Clark, M.D. Chair in Obstetrics and Gynecology. I consider the funding of the Chair one of the highlights of my tenure as Dean of the College of Medicine.

Your many honors are well deserved because of your excellence as a teacher and scholar and your superb skills in the care of women and the babies that you delivered. You are known for the astute observation of the fact that pregnancy produces two patients, the mother and the newborn baby.

On a personal note, over many years we shared many pleasant social and cultural occasions with you and your late wife Adelaide and your siblings. More recently, we enjoy our friendship with you and Alberta.

Now that you have retired, we hope that you will enjoy many happy years, you have earned them. These memoirs should be an inspiration to young people, particularly those seeking a career in medicine. It will also encourage many of the fine young men and women you trained to emulate the outstanding contributions you have made to your patients and to postgraduate medical education during your tremendous productive career.

Charles H. Epps, Jr. M.D.
Special Assistant to the President
For Health Affairs
Professor Emeritus, Orthopedic Surgery

Roselyn P. Epps, M.D.
Professor Emerita, Pediatrics

The life of Dr. John Francis James Clark has been filled with tireless compassion and dedicated service. This final chapter is excerpts of letters written by individuals whose lives he has touched while practicing medicine for more than 40 years. They represent the more than 7,000 mothers whose children he delivered, the approximate 200 young interns he's taught—many of whom became nationally renowned medical professionals, and the numerous scholars, medical researchers, and practitioners of national and international notoriety whom he knew and worked with as they made noteworthy contributions to the health and well being of black Americans, and indeed all citizens across the nation.

But perhaps more importantly, the letters are living testimonials to the legacy of Hattie Peters Clark and John Francis James Clark Senior, Dr. Clark's beloved mother and father.

The letters are also tribute to his ancestry that long ago laid the foundation for service to humankind—a West Virginia harvest bearing fruit into future generations.

As an octogenarian, I have many blessings, not the least of which is the more than 50 years of our friendship. Our personal and professional relationship has endured because of a genuine mutual respect. I am also proud of my friendship with other members of your extraordinary family. During many of our conversations, I have been struck by the numerous parallels of our background and careers. I look forward to reading what you consider the highlights of your achievements

Cyril L. Crocker, MD, MPH
Professor Emeritus and Former Chair
Department of Obstetrics and Gynecology
Howard University

In addition to Dr. Clark's clinical skills and surgical dexterity, he excelled during his career as a mentor and exemplar for his trainees and colleagues. He was always concerned with respect to economic and financial stability, moral and ethical convictions and the physical wellness (that allowed) his trainees to cope with the exigencies and demands of the program and the practice of medicine. Receptions at his home will long be remembered.

As life runs its inexorable course, we are all subject to the assaults of aging and our physical vulnerability. So, as we move on, we can only hope we have mentored a successor and lived the life. John F. J. Clark is gratified to know his trainees and colleagues are well equipped to carry the torch and to blaze the trail.

Lennox S. Westney, M.D.

There are precious few men who have had a great impact on the lives of their fellow man. One such man is Dr. John F.J. Clark, MD, FACOG. He was one of the dynamic forces of the training of highly accredited board certified Gynecologists and Obstetricians, predominantly of the minority race in the USA. I was fortunate to meet Dr. Clark, who has had the greatest influence of any mentor or teacher in my life.

"Treat all with respect, dignity, and courtesy" was his constant mantra. No great orator was he, but his actions and practices spoke volumes. In perpetuation of his philosophic underpinning as a Christian, Dr. John F.J. Clark was a teacher and a scholar, who is also a gentleman, yet a fierce defender of minority causes. He knew full well that the health of minorities here, profoundly affect the health of people every where and that is why he trained and mentored young doctors from the USA and many countries all over the world.

"The Chief" as he was known by the secretaries, students, interns and residents, took charge of all aspects of his program and commanded the respect and trust of all who worked for him. His southern pleasantries and his clever use of football as a metaphor for life, made him easily understood by many. Now he is no longer in charge of the means by which to mold the future of Ob/Gyn doctors, but his influence still prevails. Many a time he cautioned against big powers and frequently told of the poor treatment given to the most powerful men, and he warned against the bias that result in inappropriate judgment.

Long live Dr. John F.J. Clark. The legacy of his brand of caring will be passed on to future generations.

Augustus Godette, M.D.

My desire was to find a doctor with compassion, conviction, dedication, knowledge, bedside manner and a Howard University connection. When I walked into Dr. John Francis Clark's office, I knew I had found "The Doctor."

Dr. Clark was wise, kind and competent, a wonderful talker and storyteller. Not only did we have the Howard University connection, we found another one. You do not talk to him for very long before you find out his love for The Ohio State University. This was our other connection, as my stepson Buzz Thomas., his wife Patricia and I write this, my grandson, Miles Chauncey is in his freshman year and all are Buckeyes. His love for Howard and Ohio State resonated throughout our association.

Dr. Clark was very patient and tolerant of me. When we finally agreed on surgery, I saw his confident face as I drifted off. I knew I was in good hands.

As I recovered at Howard University Hospital, I looked forward to my doctor's visits. During that stay, I learned a lot about "The Chief" as attending physicians, residents and nurses were in and out of my room. As each one reviewed my chart and engaged me in conversation, knowing Dr. Clark was "My" doctor, they all related to me how he had helped them or how he had touched their lives like he had touched mine.

When John retired, I felt the loss of a very important person in my life. I used to look forward to his visits for our talks only, not the exam which I think every woman dreads. Life is good, for we became friends. Although he retired from practicing medicine, he did not retire from life, and as we all know John, "the Chief" "the Buckeye," "the Bison" is full of life and likes to be of service to his family, colleagues and friends.

I am blessed to have experienced Dr. Clark as my doctor (as you can see, I am very possessive, thinking I was his only patient—he made you feel that way). Fortunately, today he is my friend and that is a true treasure. We still talk about sports, our dear Howard University, and of course, The Ohio State University.

I am honored to share true friendship, and I wish John and his family the very best.

Sondra Norrell-Thomas
Director of Athletics
Howard University

I'm writing to say "Thank You!!" Back in April 1976, I suffered a ruptured ectopic pregnancy while at work in the lab at Howard University. Providentially, you walked into the blood bank just as I doubled over in pain. That afternoon, you removed 1500 cc of blood from my abdomen—and you saved my life.

In October 1977, you sat by my bedside in Labor and Delivery, for hours. You left me only to go home to shower and eat. You came right back to talk to me about things like the time you came to visit my parents (Lucille and Blanchard Lloyd) with your friend, Dr. John Williams.

You were sitting right there when my daughter went into fetal distress. I remember you telling the nurse to go get ready for an emergency C-Section. It was very busy that night and she told you she only had two nurses on duty. You told her two were all you needed.

That night you save my daughter's life. The umbilical cord was wrapped around her neck three times. If you had not saved my life, I would never have been around to have Dana. She is a wonderful human being.

In 1998, Dana finished the University of Maryland at College Park with a B.S. degree in chemistry. She was on a full four-year scholarship and finished with admission to several academic honor societies, including Phi Beta Kappa.

Dana was accepted into 10 medical schools—four with full scholarship offers and partial scholarships from several others. In May 2002, Dana became Dana A. Sloane, M.D. She is now doing a residency in internal medicine at the University of Maryland Medical Center. She plans to specialize in Gastroenterology.

She's an excellent physician, knowledgeable, confident, and caring. Without you, she would not be here. Thank you.

Carol Lloyd Mann Sloane

Congratulations as you are honored by the alumni and faculty of the Howard University College of Medicine.

For decades, you have demonstrated your deep commitment to protecting the health and well-being of your fellow citizens. Your efforts have helped to improve countless lives, setting an important example of service and compassion for all people. You are an inspiration to those who have the privilege of knowing you, and I am pleased to join your many friends and colleagues in commending you for a job well done.

Best wishes for every future happiness.

Bill Clinton
President of the United States of America

APPENDIX

Clark, John F. J. (1971). Adolescent Obstetrics-Obstetrics and Sociologic Implications, *Clinical Obstetrics and Gynecology: A Quarterly Book Series,* Medical Department, Harper & Row; Washington, D.C.

Clark, John F. J., Verly, Gerard P., and Johnson, Harold D., Pathogenis of Tubal Pregnancy, *Journal of the National Medical Association,* 1982, 74, 8.

Clark, John F. J., Advanced Ectopic Pregnancy, *American Journal of Obstetrics and Gynecology,* 78, 2, 1959, pp 140-350.

Clark, John F. J., and Bennett, Ridgely, Uteroabdominal Pregnancy, *American Journal of Obstetrics and Gynecology,* 81, 1, pp 298-301.

Clark, John F. J., What's on the Horizon for the Black Obstetrician and Gynecologist, *Journal of the National Medical Association,* 70 No. 5, 1978.

Clark, John F. J., and Moore-Hines, Sylvia, A Study of Tubo-ovrian Abscess at Howard University Hospital, *Journal of the National Medical Association,* 71, 11, 1979, pp 1109-1111.

Clark, John F. J., The Juvenile Parturient, *Journal of the National Medical Association,* 72, 9, 1980, pp 885-886.

Clark, John F. J., Prevented Maternal Death in Advanced Abdominal Pregnancy, printed in *Contemporary OB/GYN,* September 1978, (reprint) pp 5-7.

Clark, John F. J., Faggett, Timothy, Peters, Barbara, and Sampson, Calvin, Ulcerative Vaginitis Due to Coreopsis Glabrata: A Case Report, *Journal of the National Medical Association,* 1978, 70, 12.

Conn, Howard F. and Conn, Rex T., Postpartum Complications, *Current Diagnosis,* 6 1986, pp. 1021-1028.

Friede, A. M., Rochat, R. W., Maternal Mortality and Perinatal Mortality: An Epidemiological Perspective, In: Sachs B, ed. Clinical Obstetrics: A Public Health Perspective, Littleton, Massachusetts: PSG, Inc, 1985.

Gaither, Dorothy, and Clark, John F. J., Follow-up of Live Extra-Uterine Pregnancies, *Journal of the National Medical Association,* January 1974, 66, 1, pp 69-70, 52.

Jones, Sidney, Clark, John F. J., Anderson, Javan, X-ray Diagnosis of Advanced Extrauterine Pregnancy, Hoeber Medical Division, Harper and Row, *American College of Obstetricians and Gynecologists,* 1969, pp *578-582.*

Rochet, R W., Koonoin, L. M., and Jewett, J. F., Maternal Mortality in the United States: Report from the Maternal Mortality Collaborative, Obstetrics and Gynecology 72(1):9k.7 (1988).

Smith, J. C., Hughes. J. M., Pekow, P. S., Rochat, R. W., An Assessment of the Incidence of Maternal Mortality in the United States. *American Journal of Public Health,* 1984; 74: 780-783.

Sundari, T. K., "The Untold Story: How the Health Care Systems in Developing Countries Contribute to Maternal Mortality," *International Journal of Health Services,* 1992(3): pp 513-528.

UNICEF: *The Lesser Child,* UNICEF, New York, USA (1990) UNICEF: *The State of the World's Children,* UNICEF, New York, USA (1991).

U.S. Public Health Service, Promoting Health/Preventing Disease: Objectives for the Nation. Washington, D.C.: U.S. Department of Health and Human Services, Public Health Service, 1980:17.

Venkatramani, S. H., Born to Die. *In India Today: Living Media,* New Delhi, June 1986.

World Health Organization: Maternal Mortality—A Global Fact Book, WHO, Geneva (1991).

Rubin, Y., McCarthy, B., Sheldon, J., Rochat, R. W., J. Terry, The Risk of Childbearing Reevaluated, *American Journal of Public Health,* 1981; 71:712-716, Indiana, Louisiana, Massachusetts, Montana, North Carolina, Oklahoma, and Rhode Island.

0-595-32929-2

www.ingramcontent.com/pod-product-compliance
Lightning Source LLC
Chambersburg PA
CBHW031303280526
45784CB00004B/1969